First published in 2008
© Demos. Some rights reserved
*Magdalen House, 136 Tooley Street,
London, SE1 2TU, UK*

ISBN 978-1-84180-198-8
Copy edited by Julie Pickard, London
Series design by modernactivity
Typeset by Chat Noir Design, Charente
Printed by Lecturis, Eindhoven

Set in Gotham Rounded
and Baskervile 10
Cover paper: Arctic Volume
Text paper: Munken Premium White

# democratising engagement

Andrea Cornwall

DEMOS

# Contents

## Acknowledgements

This pamphlet has grown out of the collective work of the Spaces for Change working group of the Citizenship Development Research Centre (DRC), an international programme of research on citizenship, accountability and participation coordinated by the Institute for Development Studies and funded by the UK government's Department for International Development. It draws substantially on the introduction to a collection jointly edited with Vera Schattan P Coelho, *Spaces for Change? The politics of citizen participation in new democratic arenas*. I'm very grateful to Vera and to all my DRC colleagues. I would particularly like to acknowledge John Gaventa, whose contributions to my thinking have been significant. Many thanks also to Alison Dunn for her help in producing the short versions of the case studies from *Spaces for Change*. For their comments on an earlier draft of this pamphlet, I am grateful to Jamie Bartlett, John Gaventa and Mark Robinson.

Andrea Cornwall
April 2008

# Foreword

## Jamie Bartlett

Over the last few years there has been much discussion of the 'democratic deficit' in the UK. We are, on average, less likely to vote, join political parties, or trust our elected representatives than 30 years ago. But, at the same time, the range and size of social movements and campaigns that people are involved with has never been so broad, and over half the population says it is interested in politics. On the whole, we'd like to be involved more in politics, but cannot find easy ways to do so.

For at least a decade, democratic renewal has been a top priority for all the major parties. Since 1997 the Labour government has laid out a series of pronouncements and directives, and between 1998 and 2004 set out the bureaucratic foundations on which to build and regenerate local government, always placing citizens at the heart of their argument. In 2001, the Local Strategic Partnership was born, with requirements for representation from key public services, the business community, and the voluntary and community sector. Both the Conservative Party and the Liberal Democrats have also strongly signalled their desire to create a more dynamic civil society and a deeper culture of involving and engaging local people in democratic decision making.

But while there have certainly been successes, the overall result of these efforts is a curious paradox. A recent survey showed that only one in five Britons are satisfied with the opportunities they have to engage in local decision making, and in practice, probably fewer than 1 per cent actually do. The Power Inquiry, which was completed in 2006, found that citizens are still distant from decision making, are rarely asked to get involved and are rarely listened to.[1]

So where do we go from here?

As work like our recent *Everyday Democracy Index* shows, modern, healthy democracies must be 'everyday democracies'. They must be rooted in a culture in which democratic values and practices shape not just the formal sphere of politics, but the informal spheres of everyday life: families, communities, workplaces, schools and other public services.[2]

Over the past 15 years, Demos has carried out a wealth of participatory projects in the UK designed to engage the public in shared decision making. Time and again, our research has reinforced the importance of engaging people in their everyday lives. From using citizens' juries to inform science policy to consulting people in their workplaces, it is more important to talk to people in their everyday lives than it is to create new consultative structures and boards.

In short, we need to get beyond the bureaucratic set-up and the rhetoric, and reach beyond the immediate circles of participation into the wider reaches of the community. We need to find the everyday places of democracy that remain hidden from official outreach or consultation. We need to search for new and interesting ways to help citizens and politicians interact in effective, creative and meaningful ways in order to create progressive social change.

That's why *Democratising Engagement* is so timely. As Cornwall argues, the kind of democratic renewal that the UK so badly needs calls for creative thinking; as she puts it, 'a push to go beyond the comfort zone of consultation culture'. *Democratising Engagement* shows that there is a lot of creative thinking out there already, beyond our borders, that we can draw on for inspiration. The participatory budget from Porto Alegre, Brazil, is now well known – but there is a lot more out there. From health watch committees in Bangladesh to *panchayats* in rural India, *Democratising Engagement* draws out practical insights about what we could be doing better in the UK. Cornwall's work is especially valuable because she recognises that there are many different ways to engage people – and none of them are without difficulty. *Democratising Engagement* helps us think about how to overcome these difficulties. Of particular importance, it shows how to find better ways of engaging those who are currently most marginalised from existing consultative processes. Genuine reinvigoration of the public realm also means giving far more attention to questions of difference and enabling the most excluded to find a voice and exercise it.

As we seek to truly reinvigorate our democratic systems, we need to be willing to import ideas and learn from other countries. As we look for practical ways to move forward, this is a valuable attempt to learn from what's gone right, what's gone wrong, and how we can move forward.

*Jamie Bartlett is a researcher at Demos.*

# 1   Introduction

Citizen engagement has become an essential part of modern government. Gone are the days when the best that citizens could expect was to be told what was good for them. Governments around the world are starting to realise that engaging their citizens more in shaping the decisions that affect their everyday lives improves legitimacy, as well as the quality of public services. From Brazil's daring experiments in participatory governance, to China's recent enthusiasm for engaging the masses in deliberative forums, to the expansion of grassroots democracy in India, changes are afoot throughout the world.

Advocacy of greater citizen participation in governance is backed by democratic theorists and social psychologists who show that when participation works, it is not only good for government, it can give people a sense of belonging, a sense of control over their lives and can even be a source of happiness.[3] Yet despite promising so much, being able to reap the rewards of citizen engagement is far from straightforward or easy.

### Citizen engagement and the democratic deficit

In the UK, getting citizens more involved in different aspects of governance has become an important part of reinvigorating democracy. The UK government has recently put in place legislation that makes public involvement a statutory duty. In doing so, the UK falls in line with a growing number of countries around the world that have established legal frameworks for citizen participation.[4] And in the last decade, we've seen growing political commitment at the highest levels to giving citizens more of a voice in the decisions that affect their lives, and to engaging citizens in making government more responsive and accountable. But the UK has a long way still to go in making this promise a reality.

Since Labour came to power ten years ago, democratic renewal has been a top priority. There has been ever more intensive experimentation with methods of consultation and involvement. But what we find in its wake is a curious paradox. The Power

Inquiry's report into the UK's democratic health found that citizens are rarely asked to get involved, and rarely listened to when they do.[5] The recently published *Audit of Political Participation* suggests levels of political participation and people's sense of political efficacy are not only low.[6] They are declining. Fewer than a third of people believe 'when people like me get involved in politics, they can really change the way the country is run'. Only 12 per cent of people are considered politically active; of those, many more had engaged in individual one-off acts like signing a petition than those who had attended political meetings or demonstrations.

Levels of political disengagement are especially marked among youth and black and minority ethnic groups. Younger people are not only less likely to vote, with only 23 per cent expressing a propensity to vote relative to more than double (and rising) for their parents' generation, but so unlikely to present their views to an elected representative that barely one in 30 report having done so. Of the small fraction of the British public who are willing to get involved, the vast majority are white, middle aged, better off and better educated.

So for all the effort that has been made in recent years to engage citizens, there is clearly something missing. This pamphlet argues that addressing the UK's democratic deficit calls for more creative ways of deepening democratic engagement in the everyday work of governance. Demos has called for a radical shift in the conduct of democratic governance, one that extends beyond the ballot box to the everyday spaces in which citizens live their lives.[7] If we want to truly reinvigorate the public realm, we need to democratise citizen engagement – to open it up to much more diverse voices, experiences and possibilities. And if the kind of democratic renewal that the UK so badly needs is to happen, the public sector is going to need a push to go beyond the comfort zone of consultation culture.

## Extending democratisation

Democratising citizen engagement requires a radical shift in the way the state relates to its citizens and in people's sense of their own power to change their lives and their communities for the better. Political theorist John Dryzek offers a useful way of conceptualising this shift. He argues that democratisation is about extensions in three dimensions:

- 'franchise, the number of people capable of participating effectively in collective decision...
- scope, bringing more issues and areas of life potentially under democratic control...
- authenticity of the control,... to be real rather than symbolic, involving the effective participation of autonomous and competent actors.'[8]

Franchise has expanded as more and more opportunities are created for citizen engagement. But translating *formal* participation into *substantive* democratic engagement is another matter entirely; having a seat at the table is a necessary but not sufficient condition for exercising voice. Nor is presence at the table on the part of public officials the same as a willingness to listen and respond. 'Expansion of the number of people capable of participating effectively in collective decision' is about *capacity to work collectively*. This requires skills and experience – whether in listening, articulating an argument, negotiating and collaborating. Public servants may have few of these skills. People representing marginalised groups may also lack the skills needed to make their case or hold their ground, especially when they are up against the kinds of prejudice that are all too common in our society. Much needs to be done 'on both sides of the equation', as John Gaventa puts it, to build those capacities.[9]

Dryzek's second dimension, *scope*, focuses attention on the crucial issue of the boundaries of citizen participation – where they are set, where they are contested, and what it takes to expand the scope for citizen engagement beyond being consulted on relatively unimportant matters and excluded from the decisions that count. It urges us to differentiate between different kinds of participation and different degrees of engagement, and to be much clearer about what is at stake. Boundaries may be set by the authorities in such a way that decisions that are 'technical' in nature are black-boxed.

The expansion of scope, in many contexts, depends on vigorous citizen action. This may take the shape of contentious politics, where social movements mobilise to put pressure on the state to open up areas of policy making that are closed to citizen participation and scrutiny. It may also take the shape of incremental change from within public institutions, as progressive bureaucrats make use of the discretion that they have to lever open spaces for dialogue and deliberation. Tracing these pathways of change is important if we are to better understand how to support the expansion of this dimension of democratisation.

The last of Dryzek's three dimensions is *real* rather than simply symbolic participation of *autonomous* and *competent* actors. This dimension demands far-reaching changes in the ways most societies and governments work. First it calls for genuine devolution or sharing of powers by government, to expand what Dryzek calls *authentic* control. It requires changes in organisational culture, as well as in the attitudes and behaviour of state officials and service providers. It also demands processes and structures through which citizens can claim voice, and gain the means to exercise democratic citizenship, including acquiring the skills to participate effectively. Dryzek's emphasis on autonomy poses a fundamental challenge for contexts where the intermediary organisations that often assume the role of representatives for marginalised groups are heavily dependent on the state for funding and direction. In many ways, this dimension is more demanding than the other two, as it implies a willingness to cede control and take risks.

To begin to overcome our democratic deficit and expand democracy along all three of Dryzek's dimensions, the UK would do well to look to international experience. There is much to be learnt.

## What can international experience offer the UK?

Britain spent much of the last century exporting its institutions to other parts of the world. In the twenty-first century, it is time to reverse the flow. There is much we can learn from what other countries are doing, and doing better. Many of the good ideas for engaging citizens that are currently blossoming in the UK come from beyond our borders.

The best-known example is Brazil's inspiring experiments in participatory governance, which have caught the imagination of local governments in the UK. Participatory budgeting, Brazil's ingenious way of engaging citizens in decisions over priorities for public expenditure investment, is catching on fast. Brazilian experience shows that where municipal governments are genuinely committed to radical democracy, participatory budgeting can lead to real gains in terms of equity. And there are other benefits to be had. It can lead to increased involvement in the public arena of people who are under-represented in formal political institutions, such as women. It can bring about greater probity in government. It can also contribute to a greater sense of political efficacy as people *see* the change that their involvement brings about.

While many of Britain's former colonies have retained and reformed institutions for public administration that were put in place in the colonial era, some are also streets ahead of local government in the UK when it comes to measures to seek better representation of historically marginalised social groups. Quotas and reserved seats have been used in India and Bangladesh, for example, as a mechanism to make sure that local and national governments are more representative of women. While such measures are no magic bullet, there is a quiet revolution going on at the grassroots in these countries, as women enter politics as never before. Quite what has helped those who have never before entered the political arena to find their voice may well hold lessons for efforts to diversify Britain's political institutions.

Lessons can be drawn to further improve reforms that have been made. Many efforts at increasing citizen engagement in the UK have revolved around consultations – so much so that consultation fatigue is a symptom of modern government. This is partly because there is often a lot of talk and no follow-up. But it is also partly because conventional consultation methods can be so deathly boring. A wave of innovation in methods for needs assessment and analysis – inspired by the principle that those with direct experience of issues have much more to teach those who design policies and implement services than has ever been sufficiently fully recognised – began in India in the late 1980s and spread to the UK in the 1990s.[10] Visualisation, video and theatre techniques create an art form out of handing over the tools of research and analysis to citizens, to document their own lives and come up with solutions that work for them. Experimentation all over the UK has produced some exciting results;[11] and participatory methodologies have been used to address precisely the challenge of expanding citizen engagement.[12] Lessons from the routinisation of some of these practices in countries where the influence of aid donors, international NGOs and international financial institutions led to the proliferation of claims to be doing 'participation' can be just as valuable.

Much of this flow of experience from south to north is already happening. Some of the most innovative experiments in citizen engagement in the UK is the result of people who have worked in international development bringing home the methods and practices they had been using in Africa, Asia and Latin America – and inviting colleagues from these countries to the UK to share their experiences. Most recently, an exciting exchange event brought together local government officials and other advocates of participation from all over the world to share what they had learnt about championing participation in local governance (see box 1). The potential for these kinds of exchanges and other forms of south–north learning is enormous, in helping to inform and inspire the shift that the UK needs to make if it is to live up to the promise of recent commitments to citizen engagement.

Box 1. **Champions of participation**[13]

*In May 2007, 45 'champions of participation' from 15 countries met in the UK, convened by the Institute of Development Studies, to compare notes and strategies, and to share experiences, successes and challenges. Site visits to various locations in the UK offered international participants an opportunity to get a sense of some of the most promising experiences that the UK has to offer – and share lessons from their own experiences. It became evident from this exchange that there is a lot that the UK could learn from established and newer democracies in the southern hemisphere.*

*Across considerable differences of political, historical and social contexts, participants at the Champions of Participation exchange identified a number of core challenges that they faced:*

- *addressing negative attitudes and mutual distrust between local communities and government*
- *being more inclusive, and making sure the most disadvantaged have a voice*
- *building mutual accountability in partnership arrangements*
- *creating greater mutual understanding of the pressures on bureaucrats and citizens to deliver and engage*

· *securing longer-term sustainability of participatory initiatives and institutions*

> *These are issues that are just as much a challenge for the UK as countries with far fewer resources at the disposal of central or local government. The Champions of Participation exchange not only created an opportunity for learning, it also generated energy, enabled people to make contacts and sparked ideas that the champions could take back into their own practice.*

## From rhetoric to reality

To turn policy rhetoric about empowerment into a genuine transformation in the way the UK is governed calls for a new approach to citizen engagement – one that places a concern with inclusion and social justice at its heart. Paul Skidmore and Kirsten Bound highlight the tendency for what they call 'institutional fixes' and the inadequacy of 'institutional re-engineering as the solution'.[14] Former Demos director Tom Bentley argues:

*The solution is not simply to create more direct democracy, or to set up an ever-growing array of consultative processes divorced from the exercise of real power, but to embed both these principles – direct and deliberative – in the range of institutions through which people can express their concerns, their needs and their identities.[15]*

This pamphlet explores some of the lessons that can be learnt from experiences around the world where these principles *have* been embedded in institutions. It is written primarily for people who work in or with government in the UK. It draws on findings from a multi-country research project into the dynamics of institutionalised participation in a diverse range of different political, cultural and social contexts, *Spaces for Change: The politics of citizen participation in new democratic arenas*.[16] The focus of this pamphlet, as of the book, is on the dynamics of inclusion and exclusion, representation and voice in institutions that have become commonplace on the institutional landscape of many countries: citizens' councils, user groups, and other kinds of co-management institutions. These institutions – spaces into which citizens are *invited to participate* – form part of an expanded 'participatory sphere' that lies between the formal institutions of state bureaucracy and service delivery and the kinds of associations, organisations and informal institutions that exist within society at large.[17] It is with this participatory sphere, and the prospects it offers for democratising citizen engagement, that this pamphlet is primarily concerned.

There is much that can be learnt from 'success stories', cases where participatory governance has brought about significant changes in the ways that governments allocate resources, in citizen voice and in state responsiveness. There is a growing literature that does just this, using such cases to illustrate advances and possibilities for participatory governance.[18] The focus in this pamphlet is somewhat different. It draws largely on cases that are much more ordinary, and not particularly successful. These experiences throw up a series of dilemmas from which much can be learnt. Avoiding the tendency to extract models from one context as if they were recipes for 'best practice' that could simply be exported wholesale, this focus on the dynamics of institutionalised participation in highly diverse contexts offers a series of common preconditions and principles that are as relevant to contemporary Britain as to any of these countries.

The pamphlet begins by looking at different ways of thinking about engaging citizens in governance. It traces some of the trajectories that have led to the current policy moment, contextualising shifts in policy in Britain in relation to the broader international debate. The sections that follow look more closely at some of the preconditions for inclusive, meaningful citizen engagement through a series of case studies that reveal different dimensions of citizen (dis)engagement. Lessons from these case studies form the basis for the conclusion, which looks at what is needed to make real the democratising promise of citizen engagement in governance.

# 2 Engaging citizens

## Theory and practice

*If liberty and equality, as is thought by some, are chiefly to be found in democracy, they will be best attained when all persons alike share in the government to the utmost.*
   Aristotle

Engaging citizens in governance beyond the use of the ballot box has a long history. Pockets of experimentation as well as more widely institutionalised practices stretch back over a century in the modern state, and over millennia in earlier state formations. Known by a range of different terms – public involvement, citizen participation, popular participation, community participation, citizen engagement – talk of people participating in governance has all the ring of progressive democracy to it. Yet the history and geography of participation reveal that it has as often been used as a technique of rule as a means of giving people more of a role in their own government.[19] Much depends on who participates, what they participate in and what effect their engagement actually has on the outcomes of decisions, policies or programmes.

Like 'empowerment', 'community' and 'democracy', the word 'participation' is a normative term. It evokes and embodies ideals of how society and the polity ought to be, and of the role that people can play in government. Because there are so many different ways of thinking about these ideals, and the role and relationships of people and government, 'participation' means different things to different people. For some, it is about efficiency and the neoliberal mantra of choice; for others, it is about giving ordinary people the democratic right to contribute to decisions that affect their lives and about voice. Qualified with 'citizen', participation has a definitively democratic ring to it; coupled with 'community', it evokes a warm, inclusive feeling of people working together for the common good.

One of the hazards of today's policy language is that it is so vague and euphemistic it is not only difficult to work out what each of the terms actually means, but also what the arguments behind them are. Differences in terminology can capture differences in perspective that are useful and important to explore. At the same time, the terms people use can also simply reflect passing fashions or received usages that are never really called into question. Asking who is supposed to participate – in what, for what and why – helps bring differences in perspective into clearer view, and get beyond the feel-good language into what participation might mean in practice. Getting clearer about these dimensions of participation can help to highlight specific policy measures needed to foster more genuinely inclusive and democratic citizen engagement.[20]

This section explores different ways of thinking about participation, and what these might mean in practice.

## Making the case

Advocates have used a variety of different arguments to make the case for engaging citizens in processes of governance. They have needed to do so to convince sceptics. They have also needed to win over those whose agreement is essential to permit those lower down public sector hierarchies to invest time and effort that could be spent elsewhere, and to let the public participate in what would otherwise be closed processes. Arguments in favour of participation often emphasise it as an end in itself, an expression of political participation and what it means to be part of a democracy. But there are also arguments that stress other gains, where participation becomes a means by which to acquire them.

Three principal lines of argument can be distinguished. All appeal to aspects of today's policy discourse in the UK and in international development policy. But they have distinctive differences in emphasis, and quite different implications for where resources and energy might be best invested.

The first set of arguments turns on a vision of the democratic state in which citizen engagement is part of the very fabric of governance. A democratic state has a duty to involve its citizens in decisions that affect their lives; participation is not a favour or a privilege but a *basic right*, one that is fundamental to claiming many other rights. By engaging the public in decisions that have a bearing on their everyday lives, in figuring out what services they want and how the services they have might work better for them, participation in governance helps build a polity of and for the people. The roots of this argument lie in centuries-old political philosophy, and the writings of people like Jean-Jacques Rousseau and John Stuart Mill.

Former Secretary for International Development, Hilary Benn, made this argument in his preface to the UK government's Department for International Development's white paper of 2006, *Making Governance Work for Poor People*:

*What makes the biggest difference to the quality of governance is active involvement by citizens – the thing we know as politics… It's the only thing that can in the long term transform the quality of decision making in developing countries and the effectiveness of states.*[21]

A second set of arguments is more concerned with the contribution participation can make to creating 'better' citizens: publics that are responsive and responsible. By taking an interest in what citizens have to say and making them feel as if their views matter, by offering them information, by involving them in making sure the services they use work as best as possible and by bringing them into contact with people from the state, the state can reduce feelings of exclusion and marginalisation. This is not only about helping government to govern better. It is about helping citizens to play their part. Public involvement, then, can help address the feelings of alienation, and lack of entitlement or belonging that breeds civic disenchantment. It offers a way of (re)integrating the disenfranchised and socially excluded. And some would go as far as to argue that this work of inclusion can even reach out to those whose discontent takes expression in acts of violence such as domestic terrorism.

A third set of arguments focuses on the more pragmatic business of governing and delivering services effectively – whether by the state, the market or the voluntary and community sector. There are various dimensions to the way participation can contribute to this goal. One is as an extension of market research: a way of matching services with what the public want, of adapting existing services to take better account of expressed needs and of enlisting citizens as consumers of these services. Public involvement is, in this respect, about expressing preferences as consumers. The watchword here is choice. Another dimension of this is direct involvement in service provision, which is also referred to under the rubric of 'community empowerment'. In some contexts, this amounts to shunting the burden of the management and delivery of services from paid state officials to a vast reserve labour force of unpaid volunteers, willing to spend their time not only discussing what should be done, but actually doing it for themselves as 'active citizens'.

These three arguments – that participation produces a more democratic government, more responsible and engaged citizens and more efficient and effective programmes and policies – are not mutually exclusive. Although what comes to be emphasised varies, they are often found in some combination or other. It is their complementarity that has given participation such 'trans-ideological' appeal.[22] Communitarians and neoliberals alike might share a conviction that communities can be 'empowered' to take charge of their own development. Most of those along the left of the political spectrum believe in giving the people a voice, most of those along the right of the spectrum in giving individuals a choice. For all the potential for dissonance, it's surprising how broad a normative appeal these arguments have come to have.

There is an element of basic common sense to the argument that people who are directly affected by changes in policy and provisioning ought to be in a good position to advise government on what works for them, and what would make their lives more difficult. *Direct* engagement not only allows a whole range of people to chip in good ideas. It also gives them a stake in the outcome. It builds ownership: a sense of being part of a decision whatever happens in terms of its outcomes. Where these discussions engage people in a process of exchange and debate in which views are qualified, challenged, reframed and explained (and are not simply about people giving their view and walking away, voting, filling in a survey, or sticking a comments slip in a box), then something else happens. This process, termed 'deliberative' by political theorists and practitioners of deliberative democracy, lends a different quality to democratic governance. Cohen and Sabel suggest:

*Direct participation helps because participants can be assumed to have relevant information about the local contours of the problem, and can relatively easily detect both deception by others and unintended consequences of past decisions. Deliberative participation helps because it encourages the expression of differences in outlook, and the provision of information more generally. The respect expressed through the mutual reason-giving that defines deliberation reinforces a commitment to such conversational norms as sincerity and to solving problems, rather than simply strategically angling for advantage.*[23]

And, as Tom Bentley argues, 'deliberative conversation – channelled through institutions that in turn affect the distribution of social, economic and political power – is the form of interaction which does most to generate the forms of trust, mutual respect and understanding that democracy requires'.[24]

Participation, then, can have positive effects on politics and the polity, as well as on citizens themselves and their relationships with each other, and with the state. But much goes on in the name of participation, for precisely the reason that it sounds like such a good thing for everyone. Getting beyond the normative feel-good language calls for distinguishing a bit more closely what is actually going on when people talk about 'participation'.

## Models of participation

Many of those who work in the field of citizen participation are familiar with Sherry Arnstein's 'ladder of citizen participation' (see figure 1).[25] Developed in late 1960s urban North America, Arnstein's ladder neatly captures various forms of what she terms 'non-participation' – therapy, manipulation, informing and mere consultation – before ascending to more meaningful and engaged forms of participation: delegated power, partnership and citizen control. Her work remains as pertinent today as it was at the time. It is still the case that much of what is claimed as 'participation' hovers somewhere on the lower rungs of the ladder.

Figure 1. **Arnstein's ladder of citizen participation**

| | |
|---|---|
| Citizen control | |
| Delegated power | Citizen power |
| Partnership | |
| Placation | |
| Consultation | Tokenism |
| Informing | |
| Therapy | |
| Manipulation | Non-participation |

Source: Arnstein, 'A ladder of citizen participation'.

Arnstein's ladder is implicitly normative: the 'best' form of participation lies at the top of the ladder, citizen control. But control of what? And which citizens? What kind of power? And what are the limits of citizen control? What is in it for citizens to seek this kind of power, and the state to cede it? Other typologies help address some of these questions.

### Who participates?

Most instances of citizen participation involve only some citizens, some of the time.[26] Full participation – the participation of everyone in a community, at every step of the way – is rarely possible. This is not to say that direct democracy does not work. Swiss cantonnents practise a form of it, and the New England town meeting in the United States is one of its celebrated examples. But in practice, even the most open-ended of participatory exercises will involve only a fraction of potential participants.

A simple axis developed by Farrington and Bebbington offers a useful rule of thumb for thinking about the scope and depth of participation.[27] On one axis is the equivalent of a ladder of participation that might run from simply telling people what is going to be done through to delegating control to them to figure out how best to go about doing it. On the other is breadth of participation: from involving only a small group of people to engaging with every social group within the community. It is hard to do deep and wide participation at the same time. Yet where citizen participation has succeeded in bringing about positive change, it has often been through a combination of broad-based consultation to generate ideas, test the waters and secure legitimacy, and sustained, in-depth collaboration to shape, accompany and evaluate policy alternatives.

### Participation – in what?

Thinking back to the Dryzek's three dimensions of scale, scope and authenticity of control, the question arises: what are citizens actually participating in? Assessing the needs of the population or speaking for others? Taking part in the planning process? Debating potential policy solutions or deliberating between policy alternatives? Monitoring the implementation of policies, or evaluating programmes? Different forms of citizen engagement might be more or less suitable for each of these kinds of activities – and more or less inclusive, deliberative and democratic. A combination of mechanisms, techniques or institutions may be needed to democratise citizen engagement, each consisting of wider or deeper participation at different points in the process (see table 1).

Table 1.  **Different methods, different modes, different moments**[28]

| Needs assessment | Planning | Policy deliberation | Monitoring / oversight / evaluation |
| --- | --- | --- | --- |
| Rapid and participatory appraisal (RRA, PRA, PA) | Participatory planning | Future search | Citizens' panels |
| | Planning for real | Deliberative polling | Intermediary institutions such as sectoral policy councils (Brazil); health watch committees (Bangladesh); community groups (Bangladesh); health facilities boards (South Africa) |
| Forum theatre | Participatory budgeting | Citizens' juries | |
| Participatory poverty / wellbeing assessment | Twenty-first-century town meeting | Consensus conferences | |
| | | Citizens' panels | |
| Photovoice | | Legislative theatre | |
| Rapid ethnographic assessment / rapid assessment procedures (RAP) | | Sectoral policy conferences (Brazil) | Citizens' report cards |
| | | | Participatory monitoring and evaluation (PM&E) |

### Why participate?

Participation may bring longer-term benefits. But in the shorter term it can take a lot of time and energy. While many of the approaches to participation that have been popularised in the last decade cost a fraction of hiring a professional market research company, they do cost time, effort and money.

What is it that convinces those working in government that engaging citizens is worth it? And what is in it for the public? Why bother to participate? Sarah White contrasts four types of participation in terms of what is in it for people on each side of the citizen–state divide (see table 2).[29]

Table 2. **White's typology of participation**

| Form | What's in it for the implementing agency? | What's in it for participants? | What participation is for |
| --- | --- | --- | --- |
| Nominal | Legitimisation | Inclusion | Display |
| Instrumental | Efficiency | Costs (time, resources contributed) | As a means, to achieve cost-effectiveness |
| Representative | Sustainability | Leverage | To give people a voice |
| Transformative | Empowerment | Empowerment | As a means and an end |

Source: White, 'Depoliticising development'.

White's analysis is a useful tool for thinking through the question of where, and under which circumstances, each of the forms of participation here can create opportunities for greater citizen engagement. If the purpose of participation is to rubber-stamp already-made decisions and gain legitimacy for having ticked the participation box, then being co-opted as tokens in a situation where there is little prospect of responsiveness may call for citizens to use other tactics to gain voice. Being included even as a token can open political space that can be used to put other agendas on the table. But it can also close political space by compromising those who take part and disable them politically. This is a well-worn tactic used by powerful institutions to absorb criticism; for those who enter on these terms, exit and the use of conventional forms of protest from outside is sometimes a better way of exerting influence.

At the same time, committed bureaucrats can create the most transformative and potentially empowering participatory process – and find that there are few or no takers for it, because people have become cynical or bored, or simply don't have time to take part. Much comes to depend on the immediate and broader context: on how people feel about the government, what they expect from it, how disgruntled they feel about public service provision, how willing they feel to give up their time, how connected they feel to their communities. These shape people's expectations and willingness to get involved. If nothing much has come out of taking part in the past, there may be very little incentive to do so again.

## Trends and trajectories

Modes of participation have shifted over time. Some incremental changes can be observed, as governments and other authorities have come to recognise the limits of more shallow or instrumental forms of participation. But the most decisive factor affecting shifts in public talk and public sector practice of participation is politics. In 1980s and 1990s Britain, there was a lot of talk about efficiency, and not very much at all about social justice. More recently, and most markedly in the last few years, there has been much more attention paid to what participation can do to build citizenship and revitalise democracy.

What we might think of as 'popular participation' runs the gamut from engaging in consultation exercises to taking to the streets in protest. It is not only about people responding to invitations from the government to participate. It is also about mobilising and organising to put pressure on government, about taking part in demonstrations and other forms of popular protest, as well as seeking to influence politics by signing petitions and writing letters to elected representatives. Contentious politics continues to play a vital part in democratic governance, and in the exercise of democratic citizenship. But over recent decades, traditional forms of collective action appear to have been on the wane in many parts of the world. In this country, we have seen, on the one hand, a much more individualistic approach to political participation and on the other, a decrease across the board in citizen engagement in any kind of politics at all.

At the same time as a crisis of democratic legitimacy was brewing in the established democracies of the northern hemisphere, the wave of democratisation that swept the southern hemisphere in the 1990s was opening up myriad new democratic spaces. In both, the intersections between what was once merely the work of public administration and that of building – or renewing – democratic

vitality were never more evident.[30] Those who began from entirely
different starting points and political perspectives converged on
one common emphasis: greater participation by civil society in all
areas of governance. From the libertarian right's call for reducing
a state they perceived as bloated and inefficient, to the radical
democratic left's call for expanding the engagement of ordinary
citizens in the process of governing, participation became
everyone's panacea.

In what Brazilian political scientist Evelina Dagnino describes
as a 'perverse confluence', participation became a means to achieve
both empowerment and efficiency.[31] In the process of being put to
use in the new public management, 'empowerment' has come to
mean something quite different from the intensely political process
of mobilisation for social justice that was once associated with the
term.[32] The term has now become so elastic that it can be used to
refer simultaneously to issues as diverse as employment, creating
more civic engagement and improving the accountability of local
government.[33] We've seen a shrinking away of the original
association of the term with the least powerful in society *taking power*
and gaining the capacity to act to change their own lives, through
collective action. In its place, we hear more and more about
'communities' – as the source, resource and recourse for
empowerment.

In the UK, it was in John Major's Conservative government
that we began to see the advent of the citizen-as-consumer shaping
what was then known by a term that evokes its limited democratic
ambitions: 'public involvement'. Single regeneration budget
programmes began to open up spaces in local governance for
greater public involvement. Partnership talk has been part of
government ever since. Since 1997, the New Labour government
has invested in successive waves of regeneration, neighbourhood
renewal and community empowerment programmes. In July 2007,
Prime Minister Gordon Brown gave a major speech committing to
constitutional changes that would 'address two fundamental
questions: to hold power more accountable and to uphold and
enhance the rights and responsibilities of the citizen'.[34] Noting
that the current system of representative democracy 'can be
enhanced by devolving more power directly to the people',
Brown went on to signal what this might involve:

*First, powers of initiative, extending the right of the British people to intervene with their elected local representatives to ensure action – through a new community right to call for action and new duties on public bodies to involve local people.*

*Second, new rights for the British people to be consulted through mechanisms such as 'citizens' juries' on major decisions affecting their lives.*

*Third, powers of redress, new rights for the British people to scrutinise and improve the delivery of local services.*

*And fourth, powers to ballot on spending decisions in areas such as neighbourhood budgets and youth budgets, with decisions on finance made by local people themselves.*

*At the same time, we must give new life to the very idea of citizenship itself.*[35]

This is an exciting agenda indeed. The Local Government and Public Involvement in Health Act, which was passed a few months after this speech, in October 2007, has relatively weak legal provision of the rights Brown promised.[36] It is, however, a step forward. The challenge now is to turn this commitment into real changes in the way in which the UK is governed.

The Department for Communities and Local Government (DCLG) has laid out an Action Plan for Community Empowerment, which furthers the commitment of government to broadening and deepening citizen engagement in decision making.[37] There is clear evidence that this is needed. A survey conducted for the DCLG in early 2008 showed that 92 per cent of people surveyed thought that accountability of local councils could be improved; and only 36 per cent of people felt they were given adequate say on how local services are run.[38] Yet the forms of citizen engagement that are lauded there as evidence of increasing 'good practice' are unlikely to touch the lives of most ordinary people – especially if they are young, female, black or a member of a minority ethnic group.

Things might have improved since the local government survey of 2001 found that 56 per cent of authorities are concerned that participation exercises may simply capture the views of dominant, but unrepresentative groups. Plans to address this included 'aiming certain participation exercises (eg forum-based initiatives, user management of services and co-option to committees) at specific citizen groups or neighbourhoods'.[39] While a more recent review suggests that some progress has been made, it also signals the importance of paying more attention to social exclusion, equality and diversity issues.[40] This calls for greater investment in getting the enabling conditions right for inclusive citizen engagement. To do so, this pamphlet argues, also calls for greater recognition of the limits of targeting particular groups in this way, in the absence of broader strategies to build representation and voice.

## New democratic spaces, new democratic practices

There is now much better developed thinking about different forms of democracy than there was even a decade ago. The 'deliberative turn' in North America and Europe has gained intellectual sustenance from experimentation with a whole array of deliberative techniques and institutions. New communications technologies have fired the imaginations of those interested in new democratic designs; the possibility of virtual mini-publics e-conferencing intensively to arrive at viable policy solutions lends a whole new dimension to 'consultation'.[41]

Citizen engagement in the twenty-first century is increasingly characterised by these kinds of interchanges, and by other forms of mediation that have opened up with the new communications technologies. Those who once took to the streets to protest against policies or demand their rights may now more commonly be found in forums, consultations and committees. The landscape of democratic citizenship is changing. The expansion of the participatory sphere may have brought many more people into direct contact with government than ever before. But the political implications are somewhat more ambiguous. Citizen engagement is expanding entry into the terrain of politics by people who would probably never join a political party or take part in a demonstration. Yet questions arise about whether participation stimulates more participation, or whether participating in invited spaces absorbs and dissipates social energy.

The intensity of interaction between citizens and public servants in these invited spaces can generate greater mutual understanding, and build relationships with knock-on effects on both voice and responsiveness. But it can also result in the silencing of dissenting voices, the legitimisation of pre-set decisions and the reproduction of relations of power, discrimination and marginalisation that exist in society at large. Much depends on the ways these institutions are set up and run, on who enters them and on the broader nexus of political institutions, cultures and practices within which they are located.

The following section takes a closer look at these invited spaces, and at some of these questions. It explores what experiences of invited participation in different countries can teach us about what enables and disables effective citizen engagement.

# 3    Spaces for change?

Governments are opening up. In the past there were few opportunities for citizens to engage directly in decisions relating to public policy, or even to get basic information about public expenditure. These days there is growing transparency: in many countries, we now see the publication of budgets on the internet and in newspapers, the opening of debates within previously closed council and government meetings to the public and other measures aimed at creating more open, accountable government. A wealth of new intermediary institutions have been created in which there is far more direct opportunity than ever before for citizens and their representatives to engage directly with those who set priorities, make plans and commission and deliver services.

These 'invited spaces' are different in significant ways from the range of institutional forms that represent civil society at large.[42] They can be as much sites of contention as consensus, but these institutions are designed to promote what a Brazilian bureaucrat termed 'constructive coexistence' between social groups representing citizens' experiences and demands, and those who plan, commission and provide services. Many of these new democratic spaces have social accountability – engaging citizens directly in monitoring and oversight of public policies – as their primary function. Their location at the *interface* between state and society permits citizen voice to be effectively channelled; the presence of the state at this interface can present a better opportunity for securing state responsiveness.[43]

Taking a closer look at these institutions raises a number of questions about how they contribute towards democratising public involvement – and about what combination of design characteristics, legislation and other factors lend such institutions the possibility of realising their democratising potential. This is the focus of this section.

## Institutionalising participation in invited spaces

Invited spaces take a great diversity of forms. Some are sites in which citizens engage alongside representatives of the state in shaping policies, evaluating plans and assessing the effectiveness of programmes and projects. Others are institutions empowered to veto spending plans if they feel they will not benefit citizens. Others still are organs through which citizens get to hear about how exactly public expenditure is due to be spent – and to call to account those who do the spending. Despite this diversity they share one key family resemblance. Unlike the closed committee rooms of government, or the meeting rooms where political parties, church groups or neighbourhood associations meet those with whom they have something in common – be it ideology, faith or place – these are spaces that bring together people who might otherwise not have any occasion to be together. They are a meeting place where those who commission and/or deliver services can interact with those who represent the users of those services, or potential beneficiaries of programmes. And they are spaces that hold the potential to change the ways in which citizens engage with government, and government officials and service providers respond to those whom they are supposed to serve.

There are a number of reasons why invited spaces are especially interesting from a policy perspective. Considerable experience exists with their design and implementation. Policy makers can learn from what has gone right, and what has gone wrong. Relatively similar institutional forms exist in vastly different cultural and political contexts. There are some generic lessons that arise, especially in relation to issues of inclusion, representation and voice – the principal focus of this pamphlet. An array of institutional design principles has been developed, which can guide policy choices. While the same institutional design may have very different effects depending on the social, political and cultural context, there are elements of design that do travel.

The diversity of designs also matches with the diversity of purposes to which modern government might put efforts to broaden citizen engagement. What may be needed is a way to get some fresh thinking and ground-truth prevailing policy assumptions in people's lived experiences. Or to establish a regular feedback mechanism to monitor the quality of service provision. Other design questions follow, such as who to recruit, how to find them, what kinds of procedures and processes best fit the purpose and so on.[44] Very different people may get involved depending on whether they need to make a regular commitment, or whether they can just get involved on an ad-hoc, one-off basis.

While certain institutional designs have become ossified – especially where existing institutions have been adapted for new purposes – opportunities exist for changing the rules, introducing new procedures and strengthening the viability of these institutions through mechanisms such as training, coordination with other institutions and so on. This, again, makes invited spaces interesting to policy makers: precisely because they can be not only spaces for change, but *spaces that can be changed*.

## Spaces for change?

The expansion of the participatory sphere represents an opportunity for democratising citizen engagement. But to realise the potential of invited spaces, we need to understand better what it is that can make them effective spaces for change. Three facets can be distinguished. The first takes shape around an interest in the *rules, procedures and structures* that facilitate participation. This can be captured broadly under the heading 'institutional design', and is about the design principles that can most effectively support inclusive participation – whether in terms of internal regulations or supportive legislation.

The second concerns the *actors* involved. Understanding the mediating and mobilising role of social actors of various kinds – social movements, voluntary and community organisations, non-governmental organisations (NGOs), neighbourhood associations – can lead to greater insight into what can be done to strengthen the capacity of societal actors to engage in governance. Understanding issues of state capacity and responsiveness is equally important, whether in terms of institutional incentives, stimulating innovation or building a sense of shared commitment to inclusive, participatory governance among those who are charged with the daily job of governing.

The third concerns issues of *context, history and culture*. This is the least well developed of the three areas in the literature, but no less important than the others. It has become evident that innovations in participatory governance are not neutral technologies that can simply be exported from one context to another and be expected to generate similar results in each setting.

Getting to grips with context is about understanding better the *preconditions* for effective and inclusive participatory governance and how these can be strengthened in different contexts.

The pamphlet goes on to consider each in turn.

## Designs for democracy: new roles, new rules

According to some, the making of effective participatory institutions lies in getting the design right. Design features include not only aspects such as size, regularity of meetings and mandate but also rules about who participates, what they participate in and how they participate. Rules about who can be a member, and whether that member is appointed or elected, and by whom, have a huge impact on the extent to which these institutions are able to respond to entrenched social injustice effectively. Some institutions have quotas or other mechanisms to make sure particular people are represented – for example, social groups that have suffered persistent discrimination and a lack of representation in public institutions or those suffering from particular diseases or those working for particular kinds of organisations.

Different forms of citizen engagement deal with this question in different ways. Some approaches seek to stimulate direct engagement by and with as wide a variety of people in any given community as possible – welcoming all comers. Others seek to carefully construct a representative cross-section of the population. Contrasts are drawn by some analysts between institutions that rely on self-selection – participatory budgeting in Porto Alegre, community policing 'beat meetings' in Chicago – and those where people are recruited on the basis of representing the electorate in microcosm.[45] These 'mini-publics', as they are known, are increasingly being used to explore difficult policy choices; there have been cases where they have been used to actually make policy.[46]

In contexts where there has been significant experience with popular participation, an array of often informal rules has been developed which helps facilitate the mediation of conflict and the facilitation of inclusive deliberation. Harvard political scientist Archon Fung has produced some of the most systematic work on institutional design for deliberative and participatory governance. In a key article on the principles of deliberative designs, Fung identifies a number of key design features that help to amplify participation and inclusion.[47] He shows how certain institutional designs – involving choices over objectives, themes for the agenda, mechanisms for choosing representatives, for decision making and for the enforcement of decisions – are more or less inclined to promote legitimacy, justice or effectiveness. These dimensions do not always converge, he points out; it is hard to privilege one without sacrificing others.

Brazil has gone further than any other country in experimentation with the design of inclusive, deliberative participatory governance institutions (see box 2). Brazilian political scientist Leonardo Avritzer argues that these institutions provide an important mechanism for channelling otherwise unformed and disorganised public opinion.[48] They can harness social energy and provide a space in which citizens' diverse experiences can be given form. And they can create a sense of shared commitment to a broader societal project of social transformation in which the public are neither instruments nor beneficiaries, but active, engaged, members of the polity. This more *radical democratic* vision of participation contrasts with the neoliberal view of the citizen–consumer, or the communitarian view of 'empowered communities' doing it for and by themselves.

Box 2. **Designs for democracy in Brazil**

*Brazilian experiences with democratic innovation are some of the most exciting in the world. The contrast between Brazil's health councils and the UK's soon-to-be-abolished patient and public involvement forums could not be more marked. As the UK puts the new act into practice, Brazilian experience could prove very useful.*

*The fruit of mobilisation by the popular health movement, Brazil's architecture of participatory governance in the health sector is enshrined in the 1988 Constitution – dubbed the 'Citizens' Constitution'. This obliges municipal, state and federal governments to create and support health councils, which have a legal mandate of monitoring health policy and spending. They must approve health plans, budgets and accounts before monies are released from the federal purse. Basic health laws at each tier of government formalise the composition and mandate of the councils. Internal regulations, based on federal directives, stipulate rules of representation, the conduct of meetings and other features of design for the smooth running of these institutions.*

*The design of these institutions includes parity between representatives of the state (split between those who commission services and those who provide them) and of society. The state's most senior health officials are obliged to attend the monthly meetings of the councils. Representation of health workers runs right across the medical hierarchy and includes doctors, auxiliary nurses and community-based health workers. Representing health service users are people from social movements, such as the popular health movement or disabled people's movement, the unions, voluntary and community organisations, neighbourhood associations and particular interest groups such as religious groups. The councils are complemented by a system of participatory conferences, taking place every two to four years, at which proposals for national health policy are developed and debated.[49] Several hundred thousand Brazilians thus participate at different levels of government in the process of shaping and exercising oversight over health policy.*

*Vera Schattan Coelho from the Brazilian Centre of Analysis and Planning in São Paulo and Andrea Cornwall from the Institute of Development Studies looked at how health councils addressed issues of inclusion, representation and voice in two distinctively different parts of the country.[50] Their work revealed that even if the pathway from their creation to the councils functioning as they were intended to do is pitted with obstacles, their very existence – and the struggle to make them work – is in itself an important part of a larger process of the democratisation of public policy. Evident in both sites was the importance of both social and state actors: the effective participation of informed and articulate social actors who could take up the spaces opened up for their participation and of state actors with a personal and political commitment to making participation work. In both cases, institutional design was a key factor in facilitating the inclusion of diverse social groups.*

A growing number of countries now have legislation that makes participation an obligation of the state and a right of its citizens.[51] Laws and enabling policy frameworks in place that promote and protect citizen engagement can mean the difference between selective consultation at the convenience of the government and genuine involvement that recognises people's rights to have a say in the decisions that affect their lives. Having a right to participate means being recognised by the state and other authorities as having an entitlement to be informed and involved; making that right real calls for amplifying and channelling citizen voice on the one hand, and strengthening state responsiveness on the other.[52] Recasting the role of the public in this way – 'from users and choosers to makers and shapers'[53] – has profound implications for how citizens come to be seen by the state, and come to see themselves.

Where participation becomes a right rather than something that depends on the good will of government, the ground shifts. Those on the receiving end of public services become not just beneficiaries with needs, or consumers with preferences, but *citizens* with entitlements. Thinking of participation as a right highlights the obligations that the state has to fulfilling not only its own domestic legislation but internationally agreed human rights. These rights and obligations provide a lever for citizens to demand accountability.

## Actors: new spaces, new faces

Governments can create, institutionalise and resource invited spaces. They can use the principles of institutional design discussed in the previous section to put in place the architecture for inclusive citizen engagement. Care can be taken with rules of representation and recruitment to get the balance exactly right, thought can go into the best places and times for meetings, and expertise in facilitation can inform the way meetings are to be run. But only so much can be orchestrated. For all the designing that can be done to get these institutions right, much depends on the people who bring these designs to life.

Talk of 'civil society' and 'the voluntary and community sector' has a warm ring about it. It conjures up visions of people volunteering to benefit others. It evokes organisations that are closer to the people and more able to listen to and respond to their needs. But the use of these terms masks the diversity of organisations that lay claim to being part of these categories. Some are indeed the kinds of organisations that have the capacity, legitimacy and reach to build broad-based constituencies for change. But there are others that are far from democratic, accountable or inclusive. Much faith has been placed in the role that civic associations and NGOs can play in democratising governance. But as Neera Chandhoke points out, 'civil society' is only as civil as the society that gives rise to it.[54] A number of key questions arise: which *kinds* of civil society or voluntary and community sector organisations enable democratic citizen engagement and under what conditions do these kinds of organisations flourish and gain influence?

Current policy talk is as much about 'communities' as about the role of the so-called third sector, the myriad voluntary and community sector organisations that work with and represent those for whose benefit most social policies are intended. Democratising citizen engagement calls for going beyond feel-good rhetoric about community empowerment to face up to the complex dynamics of power relations and inequality that are inevitably part of 'communities'. Despite what Raymond Williams memorably described as the 'warmly persuasive' qualities of the word 'community',[55] it is a fact that the idyll of cohesive, caring, mutually accountable communities who simply need to be stirred and supported into playing a more active part in managing their own affairs may be a long way from reality. This is as true for the UK as anywhere else. There may be some deeply reactionary elements within communities, as there are within civil society more broadly. Those representing the state may find themselves to be the most progressive actors at the table.

This is why a rights-based approach to public policy is so important. Rather than simply calling for 'communities' to decide for themselves what their priorities are, using the principles of human rights to guide deliberations provides a way of grounding participation and empowerment in an approach that is consistent with the government's broader commitment to social justice. It enables government to defend the rights of minorities against the prejudice and discrimination of society at large, and to assert their rights to participate, as well as to support and resources. In a society like that of the UK, with homophobia, racism, prejudice against asylum seekers and Islamophobia evident in many parts of our society, this is increasingly important.

Unpacking who exactly 'the community' are raises the question of who comes to represent 'the community' in participatory initiatives and institutions. Invited spaces are also *intermediary* institutions; those who enter them become mediators between the worlds of bureaucracy and community. Those who represent 'the community' can find themselves in the middle, between the closed institutions of the state machinery and the spaces people make for themselves: privy to knowledge about the complications of the bureaucratic process or constraints on government, but faced with demands from angry people who want to see something shift. Yet this is also a powerful position to be in. Spokespeople for communities may be elected. But they are as often self-selected. The role of intermediary can easily turn into one of gatekeeper.

The wave of experimentation with participatory approaches in the last decade sought to get beyond the 'usual suspects' who would turn up to public meetings and take up seats as community representatives. The label 'the usual suspects' does a disservice to those whose experience and commitment is often such an important asset to communities. But relying exclusively on those who put themselves forward carries evident dangers of reinforcing existing patterns of inclusion and exclusion. With the expansion of the participatory sphere there are evident tensions and contradictions where elected representatives and those who represent communities speak on behalf of similar constituencies, but have very different relationships of accountability and representation with them.[56] It may well be the case that *neither* elected nor community representatives effectively represent the interests and concerns of marginalised social groups. As the case study from Bangladesh in box 3 illustrates, where little attention is given to ensuring broad-based representation, the default mode is that those who hold positions of power within any given community become its de facto 'representatives'.

Box 3.   **Who participates? 'Community participation' in Bangladesh**

*Behind the 'people-centred' Primary Health Care Declaration made in Alma-Ata in 1978 lies the expectation that if the community participates in making decisions about local health service provision there will be better health outcomes. In 1998, as part of health sector reforms, the Bangladesh government initiated efforts to enhance community participation in the public health system. Community groups (CGs) were set up in health facilities to involve the community in their management, and health watch committees (HWCs) were established to exercise citizen oversight over the delivery of services.*

*Simeen Mahmud, from the Bangladesh Institute of Development Studies, focused her research for the Spaces for Change programme on a comparison between two kinds of institutions: community groups, established by the state as co-management institutions for rural health services, and health watch committees, established and run by a NGO with the mandate of monitoring the delivery of health services.*[57]

*Mahmud's research found that mechanisms to enlist community members in the management of health care delivery in the CGs were driven more by concerns of efficiency than democracy. Representation in these CGs was by nomination or self-selection. Those who became 'community representatives' were disproportionately representative of local elites, with little contact with those whom they are supposed to be representing. Mahmud found that many community members have no idea who their representatives are, or indeed that CGs exist at all.*

*In the area where Mahmud worked, Nijera Kori, a radical NGO with a strong track record in mobilising marginalised citizens, was the implementing agency for the HWCs. A very different story emerges. Selection to the committees appeared to be more transparent, achieved through popular voting at an open workshop attended by a range of social classes. Nijera Kori suggested that half the members should be women. Representatives included people from groups of landless people formed by the NGO, professionals – lawyer, journalist, a non-government doctor, teachers – and representatives of grassroots organisations. Despite their varying socio-economic backgrounds, participants established ways of working together and were able to participate more equally. However, the absence on the committee of representatives from the state limited their ability to effect change in the delivery of health services.*

What are the lessons for effective community participation?

- *It is one thing to create a new space for participation; it is another to ensure that those who fill it genuinely represent their communities.*
- *Transparent, democratic selection and election processes are important for both legitimacy and inclusion of different groups.*
- *Communities need to be made aware that institutions exist, who their representatives are, what the roles of both institutions and representatives are, and what they might expect from them.*
- *Socio-economic or social differences can affect participants' capacity to participate or be heard; they need to be actively addressed to ensure more equitable representation and participation.*

The case of these two very different Bangladeshi institutions demonstrates a number of the points made in the previous section about institutional design. In particular, it underscores the importance of ensuring effective, inclusive representation. A lack of attention to rules of representation meant, in this case, that the people that these institutions are meant to serve are effectively excluded from participation. But there is a twist to the tale. In the kind of institution described in the first case, it is easy enough for collusion between medical staff and local elites to develop, effectively silencing any of the concerns that those who are the primary users of health services might raise. Yet while the second institution was far more inclusionary and participatory, it suffered from a critical limitation when it came to bringing about change: it lacked participation from those who were responsible for commissioning and delivering health services.

This case illustrates a broader point, one that applies as much to urban Britain as rural Bangladesh. To make use of invitations to participate, citizens need to be organised enough to understand what is going on, what is at stake and over what it is possible to press demands. For this, they need information. Recent years have seen huge strides forward in access to information, with the expansion of e-democracy, the use of the media to publish information on public expenditure, and the active use of enabling legislation to demand information. India is perhaps the most exciting place for all this at the moment, with a Right to Information act that is being used to great effect by citizens' groups to demand information and hold the government to account.[58]

But in many places, there is a lack of information on the very existence of the institutions that have been set up to enhance accountability and responsiveness. People who live in the communities that are supposed to be served by them simply don't know that they exist. For those who do, there may be little available or accessible information on what exactly they are for, and what those who represent the community within them are supposed to do. People might be selected or even elected onto such an institution and not have any idea what they are supposed to do. Sometimes they are there as tokens; all that is needed is their signature on the register to say that they are present. One obvious step towards making these institutions viable is to provide much more information about them, in forms that are accessible to all.

A further, essential, step is to provide those who represent their communities with adequate information about their roles, rights and responsibilities as representatives in these institutions so that they can participate effectively. Where rules and roles are not clear, institutions are very vulnerable to domination by professionals and those with vested interests. Those with the least power may find themselves completely sidelined. The semblance of participation can mask deep-seated forms of exclusion: where people direct their eye contact, who gets interrupted, who raises their hand and never catches the eye of the chair, who is chosen to speak first. Addressing the social and political marginalisation that perpetuates societal inequalities depends on more than making available a seat at the table and finding people to fill it, precisely because exclusion is a much more subtle process than this – it requires that we pay far closer attention to cultures of politics and to relations of power.

## Context: cultures of politics, spaces of power

Democratising citizen engagement calls for recognising that invited spaces are spaces of power in which existing societal inequalities and relations of domination and resistance can come to be reproduced. They are spaces in which styles of interaction may be borrowed from other sites in which participants engage – neighbourhood associations, political party gatherings, local government chambers and committees, protest movements – and that the cultures of politics in these institutions may be far from inclusive and participatory. They are spaces where the dominant institutional culture of government may hold sway in the way meetings are organised and run. For those who are familiar with the way things work in government, the implicit rules that govern these kinds of meetings are second nature. But they have to be acquired by those who enter these spaces if they are to be effective. Invited spaces are also classrooms, then, in which representatives of communities learn to convey community concerns in the language of technocracy.

Spaces for participation are not just management spaces. They are *political* spaces. They are also spaces of possibility, where those who lack opportunities for political apprenticeship can acquire experience. For some who take their first steps into the public sphere to join community groups or take part in a citizens' conference, participatory institutions can be a stepping-stone into the formal political arena. For others, these institutions are an arena for political engagement that can be far more enriching than formal politics. Actors within them may share significant political histories, beliefs and commitments, despite sitting on opposite sides of the civil society–state divide. Or they may hold very different political values, even if they occupy the same official positions.

Networks infused with ideological commitment, friendships, alliances and allegiances run through these spaces, complicating any attempt to disentangle the structures that are animated by these agents. Every space has a history, and elements of its past and of those of actors within it, can linger. Even as different people enter the space, these elements can pattern relationships of distrust and familiarity, collusion and contestation. There may be a lot of work that needs to be done to clear old cobwebs, and create a new basis for partnership in contexts where people have experienced round after round of consultation with no apparent results.

For all that the word 'partnership' conjures up a relationship of mutuality, where one partner is inviting the other, on their terms and holding the purse strings, the relationship is clearly not equal. Participation in invited spaces is generally on the terms set by those who create and maintain those spaces. What gets on to the agenda, and what remains off limits for discussion, may be implicitly rather than explicitly controlled by those doing the inviting. John Gaventa contrasts 'visible' with 'hidden' power; overt domination with the capacity to set the agenda before people have even arrived at the table. He signals a further dimension of power, 'invisible' power – internalised beliefs and values that mean that people do not even question the way that others treat them, nor see themselves as deserving of better.[59]

Cultures of citizen engagement that exist within any given society may take very different forms among different social groups. People with experience of dealing with bureaucracy may fail to recognise how uncomfortable it can be to enter a space with such a very different culture from the spaces in which people spend their everyday lives. Simeen Mahmud gives an example from Bangladesh of a landless woman who is a member of one of these institutions: 'I am poor and ignorant, what will I say? Those who are more knowledgeable speak more.' But while the culture of invited spaces may be one that is more favourable to middle-class professionals and local elites, who may be more familiar with the language and practices associated with the state, this is not to say that poorer people lack agency in other spaces. Mahmud draws a telling contrast with more 'traditional' forms of exercising voice, citing a female grassroots community group member: 'The educated and well-off members can debate or discuss a point in an organized way but when it comes to protesting they are usually silent and try to stay out of the scene.'[60]

Invited spaces do not exist in an institutional vacuum. Those who participate in them as citizen or user representatives may well be active participants in other spaces – members of a political party, a religious group, or a neighbourhood association. They may attend meetings on behalf of these institutions, or on behalf of the state. They may work for the state, and bring professional, bureaucratic and technical knowledge acquired in their jobs to their work as a representative. They may have had positive or negative experiences as a service user that affect the way in which they see and relate to state officials.

Whether they represent the state or civil society, people carry experiences and ways of working and interacting from one space to another. All of these experiences in other places shape the ways in which people relate to those they meet in an invited space. Someone who has experienced being talked down to by health workers is not going to suddenly see them as open, responsive and equal partners simply because they are meeting them in a different place. Those who represent the government may also identify with issues as users and citizens – they may be parents or carers themselves, they may be political party or environmental activists in their spare time.

Recognising that interactions within invited spaces are shaped by deeply rooted experiences of privilege and power, exclusion and powerlessness, is critical. Efforts to promote citizen engagement can completely ignore the need to address these dynamics. Those doing the inviting often take their own ways of seeing and doing for granted. Those who enter invited spaces may consciously or unconsciously mimic the kinds of behaviour they have witnessed in these and other spaces, in order to gain voice and influence. Simply creating a space does not mean that the space will not be filled with old ways of working, entrenched hierarchies, disabling assumptions and relations of power that reproduce the generally undemocratic institutions of the family, community and polity. Breaking with these patterns takes intensive investment in processes that restore to people a sense of their own agency as well as enable those in positions of power to recognise the limiting effects of their own beliefs and conduct.

Participatory institutions can have far-reaching effects. They can bring about the kinds of change in the cultures of politics and governance that the UK so badly needs. There is a wealth of inclusive, deliberative, institutional designs that can be used to improve the way in which the UK practises citizen engagement. But it needs to be recognised that democratic designs borrowed from other contexts are not recipes that can be expected to yield the same results with totally different ingredients. Take participatory budgeting. Closer inspection of Brazilian experience reveals some important lessons.[61] The first is that it is critical to understand better the preconditions for the successful practice of participatory budgeting – and these are more than about perfecting the technique, for all the software and other paraphernalia that is now being marketed. It is no coincidence that where participatory budgeting has made a difference, it has been in the context of radical democratic administrations. Studies have found that the democratising effects of participatory budgeting are most likely to be felt where there is a conjunction of strong progressive leadership in the municipal administration and strong social movements that are able to mobilise demands, and hold the state to account for its promises.[62] In some cities, the election of a conservative administration has meant the end of the participatory budget; in others, it has become so embedded in the life of the city that it has become part of the political culture of its citizens and very difficult for any administration to dislodge. Therein lies a second lesson. Effective participation is sustained from below, not imposed from above. Without a demand from citizens, and without a democratising impulse that is driven by their desire for engagement, there is little chance of creating the culture of participation that is needed for genuine citizen engagement.

Realising the potential of invited spaces – whether in the form of regularised institutions or more transient exercises in citizen dialogue[63] – for democratisation along all three of Dryzek's dimensions depends on challenging and changing deeply held cultural beliefs about the role of authority, of professionals and of ordinary citizens. It calls for changing the culture of formality that patterns government meetings and makes them inaccessible to those who are not familiar with established rituals. It requires changing the culture of conduct between those who may be more used to sharply demarcated hierarchies and command and control management structures and those who may have grown up in awe of professionals and afraid of revealing what they think to be their ignorance. And it means actively addressing all these and other inequalities, stereotypes and prejudices that present such potent barriers to effective participation.

The issue of representation is intimately connected to that of inclusion; and inclusion, in turn, to all three of Dryzek's dimensions of democratisation. If democratic government is to serve *all* its people, then strategies are needed to engage those with least access to political elites, resources and power. Questions of representation are fundamentally questions about democracy itself. It is to these questions that I now turn.

# 4 Who speaks for whom?

## Representation, inclusion and voice

The question of who participates – and in whose name – has come to be a growing preoccupation with the expansion of participatory governance. As new spaces for participation have opened up, new representatives have entered the scene, bringing with them a host of different ideas and practices of representation. Some reaffirm group-based forms of representation that predate the institutions of liberal democracy. Others offer entirely new ways of thinking about what a representative does, and what institutions society needs if its members are to be adequately represented in all their diversity and complexity. In the process, what it means to be a 'representative' is rapidly changing. Houtzager, Lavalle and Acharya observe:

*Citizen participation is not simply an exercise of political involvement by ordinary citizens in the policy process, but rather includes a diverse set of collective actors. This raises a significant new question in the debate on citizen/civil society participation: what forms of representation are civil society actors constructing in the new participatory institutions, and how do these new forms of representation involve ordinary citizens in policy-making?*[64]

With the creation of new democratic spaces, there has been the emergence of a generation of new stakeholders: intermediary organisations, sponsored and sustained by investment in the so-called third sector. The marketisation of social policy has produced a vast array of voluntary and community organisations that are now dependent on state contracts. While this compromises their potential role in oversight and efforts to get the state to be more accountable to its citizens, as beneficiaries of the money that flows from state coffers into service provision, it lends these organisations a proximity to the everyday needs of those to whom they deliver services.

At the same time, around the world, affiliation to what Pippa Norris calls 'mobilising agencies' – traditional mass-membership organisations that were once the principal intermediaries between citizens and the state beyond the elected representatives of the formal political system – is falling.[65] In the UK, political

participation has become more individualistic; the combination of
the rise of 'credit card activism' and extremely low levels of political
party membership have left the political landscape denuded of the
kinds of institutions that can effectively channel dissent into
constructive engagement with the state.[66] For all the designing that
can be done to create inclusive institutions, much depends on who
enters these newly created spaces – and on what they bring with
them. One of the things they bring is a range of different
understandings of their role as representative, as the case study in
box 4 illustrates.

Box 4.    **In whose name? Representation in São Paulo, Brazil**

*How do those who represent organised civil society in Brazil's
numerous participatory institutions see their role as
representatives? Peter Houtzager and Adrian Gurza Lavalle's
work – with collaborators Arnab Acharya and Graciella Castello
– explores some of the implications of new and emerging forms of
representation in participatory governance. A survey conducted
in São Paulo among civil society organisations generated six
principal justifications:*[67]

- electoral: *because being elected authorises representation and,
  simultaneously, secures accountability*
- proximity: *because the organisation's degree of closeness,
  solidarity and empathy with their public, and being sought
  after by those publics for that reason, legitimises representatives as
  a demonstration of their genuine interest and role as
  representatives*
- services: *because the organisation provides services to people, it
  knows what people need (in implicit contrast to traditional
  representatives who neither know nor serve those whom they
  represent)*
- mediation: *because the organisation opens up access to public
  decision-making institutions that otherwise would remain
  inaccessible, so as to make claims in the interest of its public*
- membership: *because the organisation has been formed to
  represent its members*
- identity: *because the organisation is of members of a particular
  social group it can speak for them and act in their interest*

*The electoral, membership and identity-based arguments are familiar ones from the literature on political representation, and have the oldest historical roots. But they were the least common among the civic organisations interviewed. The most common argument – the 'mediation argument' – was made by over a third of the respondents. It is related to recent democratic reforms to provide citizens greater access to, and control over, the state and to the new roles civil organisations are undertaking. The prominence of the mediation argument, as well as its common rival the proximity and service arguments, suggests that the new role of civil organisations in contemporary polities may be contributing to an important change in the symbolic construction of democratic legitimacy.*

Effective participation depends on having effective participants. The considerations raised in the previous section suggest that closer attention needs to be paid to the extent to which these new democratic spaces are transforming or reproducing old undemocratic relations. In contexts where deeply embedded patterns of social inequality exist, there is every possibility that culturally entrenched relations of prejudice and power are simply reproduced in any new spaces that are created – unless active attempts are made to mitigate their effects. Ordinary citizens may find that these are less *spaces for change* than spaces in which their marginalisation is reaffirmed, as the example from South Africa in box 5 shows.

Box 5.  **Social change and community participation in South Africa**

*Today's possibilities for citizen participation in South Africa are deeply shaped by the country's apartheid history. There were no legal rights or avenues for black participation and political self-governance until 1994. Since then, there has been 'transitional governance' and demands for deep social change. In this context community participation is literally synonymous with legitimate governance.*

*John Williams, from the University of Western Cape, South Africa, researched the case of citizen representation on health facilities boards (HFBs) in the Western Cape as part of the Spaces for Change programme. HFBs were established to ensure greater community participation in the provision of healthcare services at grassroots level.[68] The Health Facilities Boards Act makes it explicit that community representatives must constitute at least 50 per cent of a HFB. Theoretically this means that communities are able to influence the formulation, implementation, monitoring and revision of hospital business plans, hospital staffing and the quality of hospital services.*

*One of the most pressing challenges in the HFBs is the dramatic under-representation of black South Africans. Williams' analysis of two HFBs in the Western Cape shows the racially skewed nature of the HFBs and explains why black people in general do not participate. Historically, whites have dominated governance institutions in South Africa, including hospitals and health clinics. Election procedures of HFBs favour literate and more influential members of a community at the expense of poorer, largely illiterate members. And a culture of deference to professional authority undermines real dialogue and the empowerment of black communities.*

**What steps can be taken to improve the representation of excluded people?**

· *Improve communication through the use of more direct forms of communication like rallies, door-to-door visits, street theatre etc.*
· *Open up the dynamics of these new participatory spaces to engagement – including creating space for discussion of who has authority over the agenda, dynamics of authority and deference, inflexibility and protocols.*
· *Change rules of representation to ensure that there is representation from all users, including measures such as the reservation of seats for particular excluded groups.*

Where institutional design meets analysis of the actors who are involved in participatory institutions, it becomes evident that changing the rules – particularly rules of representation – might well make an immediate difference in creating the basis for more equitable representation. Taking a closer look at the dynamics of participation in practice shows that while design features like quotas or reserved seats may be a necessary step towards getting a critical mass of under-represented social groups into the political arena, this does not directly translate into substantive participation (see box 6). Societal prejudices and assumptions can be compounded by a relative lack of assertiveness, articulateness, consciousness and clout. Tackling these issues becomes a priority if these kinds of institutions are to contribute to democratising decision making over public policies and institutions.

Box 6.    **Gendered subjects**

*In the last two decades, the Indian state has created a variety of institutional spaces at the village level to encourage lower-caste and tribal groups and women to participate in governance. Ranjita Mohanty from the Society for Participatory Research in Asia carried out research as part of the Spaces for Change programme.[69] Her study illustrates how, in this context, the physical presence of women – made possible by legislation that requires all institutions of local governance,* panchayats, *to reserve a third of their seats for women – was not matched with opportunities to exercise voice or influence.*

*Mohanty looked at the presence and absence of women in three institutional spaces: health and watershed development institutions and* panchayats *– units of local governance at the grassroots level.* Panchayats *have a constitutional mandate to encourage the political participation of women, and reserve a third of their seats for women. Watershed committees are also obliged to include women representatives. Yet it was only in the mother-and-child-focused health committee that women were able to participate in any meaningful way. Formal participation in the other two arenas did not translate into substantive engagement. Women endured meetings in silence, reduced to mere signatories, or were actively sidelined if they did speak up.*

*When women are asked to join committees or* panchayats, *it is often to meet procedural requirements. Women members are seen as decorative; who among women in a community will stand for election is a decision rarely taken by women themselves. Rather than political empowerment or expanding women's political imagination, these institutional spaces commonly end up reproducing stereotyped identities of women. Women may find themselves overwhelmed by the barriers they face to exercising voice and influence, resigning themselves instead to the tokenistic roles they are given by men. It becomes hard for them to organise on their own to negotiate and claim their rightful stake in local participatory institutions.*

### What would help women to participate?

- *Experience of participation in other spaces, such as those created by local organisations, associations of movement, enables women to gain the skills and confidence to speak in public.*
- *The state can play a role in supporting women's participation by not only putting enabling mechanisms in place (such as reserved seats or quotas for women) but ensuring compliance with them, and actively facilitating women's participation within these spaces.*
- *Where women have participated in leadership training, consciousness-raising and other processes aimed at enhancing their political agency, they are much more able to make their voices heard.*

An enabling legal framework needs to be complemented by other strategies if it is to foster inclusive participation. Securing seats within institutions like councils or committees for traditionally excluded groups through quotas or reservations may be a necessary condition for their inclusion, but is often not sufficient for their *substantive* participation. Mobilisation can create new leaders who can represent community or group-based interests; this can be one of the most promising routes to exercising voice. But those with least societal power are often the least able to organise, mobilise and put themselves forward as a social group. How, then, can their needs and interests be most effectively represented? What is needed to turn a place at the table into a real opportunity to shape the agenda?

Chaudhuri and Heller argue that a critical shortcoming of the debate on deepening democracy is that it has assumed individuals are equally able to form associations and engage in political activity.[70] This, they argue, ignores fundamental differences in power that exist between social groups:

*If this is problematic in any less-than-perfect democracy (and there are no perfect democracies) it is especially problematic in developing democracies where basic rights of association are circumscribed and distorted by pervasive vertical dependencies (clientelistic relationships), routine forms of social exclusion (eg the caste system, purdah), the unevenness and at times complete failure of public legality, and the persistence of pre-democratic forms of authority.*[71]

If the skills to participate are just that – skills that might need to be acquired by those who have rarely had opportunities to engage in the public arena – is it enough to expect participants to acquire them for themselves? There is clearly a role that intermediary organisations, and indeed the state, can play in that process of learning, and of mobilising people to make use of invitations to participate. But what is that role – and where do its limits lie? And how can governments do better in engaging groups that have historically been excluded from playing any part in determining public policies and service provision?

# 5 Towards inclusive representation

There are different perspectives in the extensive literature on representation as to how best to ensure the inclusion of less organised and historically marginalised social groups. Some argue for a more direct democratic approach: that participatory institutions should be open to everyone who wants to participate. There are those who point out the risk that self-selection may favour those with the most resources, and who propose methods of random selection that seek to mirror the makeup of the population at large.[72] Others argue for a focus less on methods of selection and more on incentives for participating.[73] And others again believe a process of mobilisation is what is needed to create the basis for marginalised social groups to represent themselves.

Jane Mansbridge argues that in cases where there are no clearly identifiable positions and where there is strong distrust for the state, historically marginalised social groups need to be represented directly.[74] One way of addressing this is to make sure there is someone from these groups at the table; that is, rather than have someone speaking for people with, for example, a particular disability, someone with that disability is asked to represent others like them. Such a 'politics of presence', Anne Phillips suggests, provides a number of challenges to existing patterns of exclusion and marginalisation.[75] First, there is a symbolic value in having members of an excluded group present at the decision-making table. Second, it opens the decision-making process and creates the conditions for a more vigorous advocacy of their interests. It can facilitate a politics of transformation by giving previously excluded groups the time and opportunity to construct their political preferences and express their concerns for themselves. But it also runs a number of risks, among them tokenism and the possibility that those who come to speak for a particular social group end up becoming a 'professional participant', rather than using a seat at the table to open space for and reach out to others.

Addressing the issues of representation raised in this pamphlet is not only about ensuring better, more inclusive rules of recruitment, election or enlistment. It is also not just about getting a greater diversity of actors around the table. It is also about recognising that the cultural styles of dialogue and forms of representation that are to be found in invited spaces may depart to such a degree from those with which some participants are comfortable, that entirely different structures and processes might be required so as to enable them to participate. But even the best-made designs have their limits, if they assume a monoculture rather than provide for cultural differences in modes of representation, dialogue and deliberation, as the case in box 7 shows.

Box 7.  **Healthy futures?**

*The Romanow Commission was established in April 2001 by the Canadian government to engage Canadians in a national dialogue on their health system. An extensive consultation process included expert reports and panels, consultations and deliberative Citizens' Dialogues with statistically representative groups of 'unaffiliated' citizens using a sophisticated deliberative technique, ChoiceWorks. In their study for Spaces for Change, David Kahane and Bettina von Lieres found that while some Aboriginal people were included in the dialogues, the outcomes did not reflect Aboriginal health issues.[76] They explore why this was the case. Their analysis suggests that the design was a perfect fit for a society which prizes the sovereign individual, but not for societies in which forms of group-based representation are culturally dominant. Aboriginal people participated in all sessions, but were typically very quiet. Two localised ad hoc attempts to hear more Aboriginal voices – though creating a small separate group and recruiting additional Aboriginal people to sessions – had little effect.*

*These experiences point to the difficulty of engaging and empowering members of marginalised groups within invited deliberative spaces and to the limitations of piecemeal innovations in surmounting these difficulties. This was a failure to overtly engage with the complex politics of representation. Who needs to be at the table and in what numbers? How do dynamics of exclusion and marginalisation get managed within the process? Giving Aboriginal people a more influential voice would have required changes to the basic structure of the dialogue, thus challenging the individualistic premises of the method. Design choices are critical in enabling marginalised groups to negotiate the complex politics of recognition and representation.*

What would enable marginalised groups to participate?

· *Giving participants more scope to define the terms on which they deliberate, the issues they address and the form that the deliberation takes, can foster more genuine participation on people's own terms.*
· *Treating participation as a process in which people learn as they go along, rather than one that is oriented at hard and fast conclusions, can favour different modes of making contributions.*
· *Supporting the creation of separate spaces in which members of these groups can reflect on dynamics of power, negotiate common agendas, strategies and identities, and provide room for the internal complexities of perspectives to be dealt with democratically and deliberatively.*

Designing processes of inclusive participation that do not simply impose the terms and cultures of politics of the majority on minorities is a challenge. In the absence of spaces of their own making, marginalised groups may lack the opportunity to recognise their own distinctive needs, create a shared agenda and gain the capacity and confidence to act in the public arena.

What, then, would it take for these groups to gain meaningful opportunities to participate?

## Of other spaces

Feminists have argued that to be politically effective within the public arena, marginalised groups require their *own* spaces in which they can construct and consolidate positions, gain confidence to speak and gain access to a broader constituency of support.[77] Nancy Fraser talks of '*subaltern counter-publics*'. Jane Mansbridge argues that 'laboratories of self-interest' may be needed to enable historically marginalised groups to build positions as well as to gain greater legitimacy to be able to voice their demands within, and outside, participatory institutions.[78]

Social movements play an especially vital role in creating these kinds of spaces. But voluntary and community organisations and the state can also make an important contribution to broadening representation and enabling marginalised groups to find and exercise voice. Such support includes training in public speaking, awareness-raising on entitlements and rights, consciousness-raising work that enables people from marginalised groups to recognise their own issues in their own ways and find the inner and collective power to act in the public arena, and the provision of meeting spaces and other kinds of logistical and financial support for particular groups.

One important lesson from experience is the delicate balance between fostering the creation of autonomous spaces by historically marginalised groups, and what happens when well-intentioned outsiders make and shape those spaces *for* others. NGOs and voluntary organisations may be anxious to help those they seek to help to represent themselves, but may also end up speaking for them and limiting their opportunities to represent themselves. There are other implications. Creuza Oliveira, leader of the Brazilian national federation of domestic workers, recalls the contrast between the meetings convened by a Catholic priest to mobilise domestic workers and what happened once they succeeded in getting a small grant from an international NGO to get a place of their own to meet.[79] It was not just what they were then able to put on the agenda for discussion – sexuality, contraception, abortion and other issues that simply could not be discussed within the space provided by the church. It was about having a place to be: a place to laugh together, sing together, plot and dream together; a place outside the gaze of officials, where people can be who they are rather than having to adopt a way of relating that belongs to another world. From these spaces of their own making, people can gain the confidence and collective strength to act.

In theory, both direct and deliberative democracy foster processes in which people in all their diversity come together to express their views and seek solutions. In *practice*, people often arrive in these spaces with preformed agendas that can be very hard to shift. The rub is that for social movements and for certain more issue-oriented organisations, it is these agendas that constitute their platform. Their own legitimacy with their constituencies depends on defending and advancing a position. Social movement theorists suggest that the creation of oppositional consciousness – 'us' versus 'them' – is often key to effective mobilisation.[80] Political theorist Chantal Mouffe argues:

*The political is from the outset concerned with collective forms of identification; the political always has to do with the formation of an 'Us' as opposed to a 'Them', with conflict and antagonism.*[81]

This poses challenges when it comes to engagement in invited spaces. These are spaces for consensus, and for compromise; as intermediary spaces, they can also put the intermediaries who enter them in positions whereby their own legitimacy comes to be compromised.

## The paradox of inclusion

Arguments for the inclusion of socially marginalised groups rest on an assumption that if only these groups were better represented and more able to exercise voice, then their participation would lead to fairer public policies that would better serve their needs. But sceptics would argue that this involves a leap of faith. The cards are stacked against the possibility of such groups gaining much in the way of voice or influence. And, as John Dryzek suggests, inclusion brings risks as well as opportunities: while such groups may be permitted to participate, unless their agendas coincide with those of the state they may stand little chance of influencing outcomes.[82]

If, as Dryzek suggests, there is a price to be paid by such groups for inclusion, what is at stake – and what implications does this have for democratising citizen engagement?

In settings where there are so many participatory initiatives and institutions, organisations need to be very strategic about whom they put forward as representatives and how much energy they devote to invited participation, and how much to stimulating other forms of participation at the grassroots. Taking up a seat at the table may dampen activism, not least because of the time and energy that engagement can take. An evaluation of Neighbourhood Renewal found both an expansion of opportunities to participate, and evidence of emerging fatigue and confusion as a result.[83] People may find themselves spending hours in meetings in which they have little chance to speak, or be heard.

Equipping people with the skills to negotiate within a system that continues to disadvantage them may give them some tools but, as Audre Lorde observed, 'the master's tools will never dismantle the master's house'.[84] Learning the language and styles of argumentation of the white, middle-class men who have traditionally dominated public institutions may give people from other social groups some advantage. But this in itself may do little to change these institutions and make them more inclusive of diverse forms of expression, styles of reasoning and testimony, and forms of dialogue and negotiation. For this, much more far-reaching changes to the political system are needed.

Energies can be absorbed into negotiating around minutiae and seeking small concessions rather than being involved in decisions on the issues that really matter – which might be off the agenda. Activists complain of spending their lives running from one forum to the next meeting. They ask: What are we *not* doing by spending all this time responding to invitations to participate? Batliwala and Dhanraj raise a wider caution about the extent to which getting drawn into 'backwater' minutiae at the community level can defuse political energy that people might otherwise have been putting into mobilising to address the bigger issues affecting their lives.[85] The irony, then, is that while invited participation may stimulate more participation, it may also detract social energy from engagement with issues that are not on the agenda in invited spaces.

## Engaging the state

More attention has been given to how to stimulate and support citizen participation than to what is needed to do the same for those who represent the state. Yet it is now evident that one of the most decisive variables in making participatory governance work is the engagement of responsive, supportive state actors. It stands to reason. Citizens can mobilise to press their demands, but to get anything to change in the way services are delivered, those who plan and deliver those services have to be not only part of the conversation but committed to following through.

What is it that motivates state officials to participate and to follow through decisions arrived at in these spaces? What makes bureaucrats amenable to long and convoluted deliberative processes that take up inordinate amounts of time, rather than resorting to quicker and more authoritarian decision-making processes? What incentives motivate officials to invest in these spaces and what do they get out of participating in them?

Getting politicians and bureaucrats to back the kind of public involvement that goes beyond the usual 'we tell–you agree' variety rests on a number of factors. One factor is public opinion; politicians are more likely to respond if they feel that there is going to be political capital to be made, or where there is pressure from the public and the press. Another factor is what they themselves believe in, their own values and political projects. Where these coincide with political opportunities for expanding citizen participation, politicians and senior civil servants can play an incredibly important role in legitimising as well as lending support to public involvement. In some cases, politicians have gained credibility and improved their electoral prospects by publicising their passion for participation. In others, senior civil servants have advanced their careers by championing innovation in governance, and by being able to show results.

While in the past there was little incentive within public service for participation, these days the watchwords are innovation and empowerment. Times are changing. Public servants who promote an agenda of responsive, accountable government that genuinely seeks to involve citizens can find themselves swimming with rather than against the tide. But they are still in the minority. Visionary leadership and a willingness to take risks and experiment is what it has taken to make change happen in the pockets of innovation that we now see around the UK. But mainstreaming participation calls for nuts and bolts organisational changes across the board that encourage and reward public officials for following through on policy commitments on participation. For this, clear guidance is needed and an appropriate combination of incentives and sanctions.

State support is a vital lifeline for fledgling groups with no resources to sustain themselves. The state has a vital part to play in promoting and protecting the rights of minorities, actively challenging and combating racism, homophobia, sexism and other forms of discrimination and abuse, and guaranteeing to all the right to participate. But well-intentioned but unreflective behaviour on the part of those who work for the state can have quite the opposite of the effect it is intended to produce – disabling citizen engagement. As Marian Barnes' work suggests (see box 8), enabling marginalised groups to develop their own agenda and the means of communicating it for themselves may call for working with those who are supposed to be doing the listening rather than coaching these groups in the right ways to talk to get heard.

Box 8.      **Whose spaces? Local action for health in the UK**

*Marian Barnes from the University of Brighton looked at a community health forum in the UK, set up by residents in an area with a strong tradition of community activism.*[86] *When residents discovered that the health authority was planning to close their health centre, they mobilised and undertook research to demonstrate that the health centre was needed. The campaign was successful. Residents decided to continue working to improve health services in the area. Six years later, the group decided to bid for funding from the National Lottery for a Healthy Living Centre. To qualify they had to reconstitute themselves as a health forum.*

*The group had moved from oppositional action to trying to work in partnership with the health service. Their strong sense of 'we' became more muted and diffuse; they struggled to retain a committed membership. Their interactions got bogged down in bureaucratic details. This constrained creativity and dampened enthusiasm generated by direct involvement in community-led research. There was considerable expertise and knowledge within the community, but this was not a priority in comparison to the technical knowledge needed to put together a funding bid. Discussions were highly task-focused and technical.*

What are the conditions needed to make the most of citizen participation?

· *Officials need to develop skills for working creatively with conflict rather than try to deny it or close it down.*
· *Officials themselves need to be supported and rewarded for these skills.*
· *There needs to be space for multiple forms of expression – both emotional and rational – and for diverse ways for people to*

*express themselves. This can be achieved through good facilitation, but can also be 'squeezed out' when an external agenda is imposed.*

· *The rules of the game between citizens and government officials need to be negotiated and adhered to in order to develop mutual trust. This is easier to achieve when people have the opportunity to develop collective awareness.*

· *Autonomous organisation and 'free spaces' not affiliated to state institutions are important places to try out new ways of thinking and action before engaging with officials.*

If part of what participation is about is what Arnstein calls 'delegated control'[87] – that is, the state being willing to delegate control to citizens – then public servants need to get a lot better at trusting in the process and letting go. This can be incredibly difficult, especially when there is a lot at stake. There are trade-offs and interactions between measures that democratise public involvement by including more people in more decisions and those that seek to improve the quality of democratic deliberation and the fairness and viability of the solutions that arise from it. Public policy is a political issue. Unpopular policy measures may be needed to ensure equity. Governments need to balance the difficult issue of boundary setting: determining what can be decided jointly with the public or through delegated authority to citizens themselves. Very real tensions arise between short-term and long-term solutions, between inclusiveness and effectiveness, between struggle and negotiation.

Yet it is vital to recognise that participatory governance is as much about stimulating the democratisation of society and about democratic renewal as about improving service delivery. It is about positioning the state as a supportive partner in social transformation, one that is willing to take the lead in creating a new culture of participation. Care needs to be taken not to erode a sense of ownership and to diminish social energy by simply absorbing citizen-initiated institutions within the bureaucratic apparatus of the state. Such support needs to begin with what would best support citizens to expand and deepen their own engagement.

## Transforming power

Participatory governance institutions are growing in scope and scale. Citizens have far greater opportunities to get their opinions heard and influence decisions. But a question that recurs throughout this pamphlet is this: Will this contribute to changing the status quo for those who have historically been marginalised politically and economically, and who continue to face potent forms of discrimination – women, black and minority ethnic groups, lesbians, gay men, bisexuals and transgender people?

Some would argue that it is only when those who are excluded from power have organised themselves to make demands on the state that they get to be heard. There is ample evidence from all around the world that rights are rarely simply handed to people; they are won through struggle.[88] And this is not a once-and-for-all struggle to get a seat at the table, or recognition as a group with specific needs and interests. It is an ongoing process of contestation that is waged anew in each new institutional space, as new people enter and new configurations of power and interests emerge.

Mobilisation creates a sense of identification with an agenda for change, raises people's consciousness of their rights, and lends them collective strength and representatives who can speak for them. It can also provide avenues for political apprenticeship that are simply not available within the formal political system. Demands for a seat at the table can turn invited spaces into what Marcus Mello has called 'conquered spaces',[89] where opportunities to participate are actively claimed from the state rather than simply granted from above. Nancy Fraser usefully frames struggles for rights within the rubric of redistribution, recognition and representation.[90] Struggles for recognition and representation have made substantive contributions to confronting societal prejudice by confronting demeaning and discriminatory representations of women, black people, people with mental illness and other groups that are on the receiving end of prejudice. Struggles for redistribution – the landless people's *Movimento dos Trabalhadores Rurais Sem Terra* in Brazil, the Treatment Action Campaign in South Africa, the *dalit* movement in India – have transformed the prospects of some of the most marginalised people in the world. Making use of the media, the internet, the courts, direct action and popular protest, these movements have secured real material gains, and substantive changes in social policies.

Whether these gains could have been negotiated within

invited spaces without the possibility of mobilising outside them to put pressure on the state is an open question. A dual strategy may be most effective in relation to invited spaces: taking up places inside them, while continuing to exert pressure from outside.

Creating the preconditions for effective citizen engagement is, then, not simply about getting the rules right, nor only a matter of getting a greater diversity of actors into invited spaces. It is also about redressing entrenched cultures of politics and relations of power. These are unavoidably *political* issues. The bottom line remains that enabling people to negotiate more effectively in the context of unjust power relations is one thing, and addressing the underlying structural issues that perpetuate inequalities and marginalisation is another. It is no coincidence that where citizen engagement in invited spaces has led to a more equitable distribution of resources or to policies that address issues of inequality and discrimination affecting marginalised social groups, it has been in the context of political administrations run by parties on the left of the political spectrum.

In the UK, we have seen shifts of policy discourse in recent years from an emphasis on the active citizen empowered by choice to communities empowered by collective responsibility. It is perhaps time for a further shift towards a more rights-based vision of citizen engagement, in which citizens and communities empower themselves by exercising their rights to participate in governance. For this we need stronger legislation than the current commitment to inform, involve and consult where the authorities deem necessary. And we need far greater attention to be paid to developing new ways of engaging citizens that bring the democratic process closer to their everyday lives – and to changing the rules of the political game to permit a far more diverse set of possibilities for engagement.[91]

# 6 Democratisation and empowerment

## Futures possible

*The old saying that the cure for the ills of democracy is more democracy is not apt if it means the evils may be remedied by introducing more machinery of the same kind as that which already exists, or by refining or perfecting that machinery. But the phrase may also indicate the need of returning to the idea itself, of clarifying and deepening our apprehension of it, and of employing our sense of its meaning to criticise and remake its political manifestations.*
John Dewey[92]

If we have learnt anything from the efforts that have been made in the UK in recent years to address the democratic deficit, it is the importance of *democratising* citizen engagement. Much has been vested in finding new ways of engaging citizens, but much still needs to be done to expand democracy along all three of Dryzek's dimensions – franchise, scope and authentic control.

The Spaces for Change project's findings suggest that democratising citizen engagement depends on a *conjunction* of factors, rather than one factor alone:

· strong, active social movements and civil society organisations with broad-based popular support that can effectively take up invitations to participate and make demands 'from below'
· strong, enabling leadership and committed state officials, backed by enabling legislation that makes citizen engagement a statutory obligation, budgets to provide infrastructure for participatory institutions, capacity development for those who take part in them and resources to finance follow-through actions to demonstrate responsiveness
· institutional designs that optimise participation and representation of society in all its diversity, foster deliberation rather than simply weak forms of consultation, and engage those within the state who have the power to affect outcomes
· social energy, trust and demand for participation and actions that foster a democratising impulse in society at large – whether in terms

of new understandings of citizenship that encourage citizens to engage in shaping the polity that they are part of, rather than remaining passive beneficiaries or consumers of services, or new opportunities for political participation that go beyond increasingly individualised forms of engagement

Looking at some of the factors that enable or disable participation (see table 3), it is clear that there are significant challenges for the UK in making real the commitment that this government is making to participation and empowerment.

Table 3. **Enabling or disabling participation: a summary of factors**[93]

| Enabling factors | Disabling factors |
| --- | --- |
| Political context | Political context |
| Strong social movements able to hold state to its promises | Weak or no social movements |
| High levels of political awareness | Political apathy |
| Voluntary sector/civil society relatively autonomous from government | Authoritarian regime with minimal investment in consultation |
| Political regime committed to social justice | Neoliberal regime with minimal investment in public sector |
| Significant public sector provisioning | Significant and increasing reliance on voluntary, community and private sector for service provision |
| Trust in the political system and state institutions | Widespread distrust of the state |
| Strong sense of citizenship (as entitlement and belonging) | |
| Legal framework | Legal framework |
| Existence of legal or constitutional rights to participation | Weak or absent provision of rights to participate |
| Existence of complementary rights (ie right to information, rights of redress) | Lack of additional supportive legislation or conditionalities that qualify or contradict statutory duty to engage citizens or citizens' right to participate |

71

Table 3.  **continued**

| | |
|---|---|
| Legal framework continued | Legal framework continued |
| Sanctions for non-compliance | Lack of sanctions for non-compliance |
| Clearly specified means and mechanisms for redress | Lack of clear means and mechanisms for redress |
| Existence of statutory duty to engage citizens in policy processes | |
| Bureaucratic context | Bureaucratic context |
| Political will at the highest level of the bureaucracy and strong leadership | Lack of political will among senior managers |
| Widely shared commitment to citizen engagement | Widespread scepticism about benefits of citizen engagement |
| Consistent policy directives, joined-up government | Contradictory policy directives coming from different parts of government |
| Incentives and sanctions | Lack of incentives and sanctions |
| Dedicated support (information, mentoring, coaching, trouble-shooting) | Lack of information and support for implementation |
| Resources to create and maintain infrastructure to support engagement | Lack of resources to support citizen engagement or implement initiatives |
| Sufficient room for manoeuvre to take risks, be responsive and experiment | Lack of support or scope for experimentation |
| Adaptive, flexible approach to implementation | One size fits all models |
| Time to make mistakes and learn from them | Pressure for rapid implementation |
| | Disbursement and performance pressure |

Lessons from international experience emphasise the role that the state can play in stimulating and supporting citizen engagement. Legal frameworks are important. So too are systems of incentives and sanctions. But political will, genuine commitment to democratising governance, and the visionary leadership needed to make the kind of transformations in cultures of politics and bureaucracy are absolutely critical. If governments are serious about involving their citizens in government, then they need to be willing to open up the process of setting policy agendas, prioritisation and policy deliberation, and committed to following through on outcomes of these deliberations. They also need to be willing to set aside resources to establish and maintain these institutions, such as for an administrator to coordinate and keep a record of meetings that can become an institutional memory, money to hire rooms, pay for transport and other associated costs, and so on. And they need to be able to call on flexible, responsive funding that will allow them to act on quick wins, as well as the budget to plan longer-term initiatives, with which to demonstrate to citizens that engagement can lead to tangible actions.

One of the most evident shortcomings of existing attempts to engage citizens is precisely in relation to who gets to participate and whose voices count. Those who have the least material and symbolic resources also have the least opportunity to influence the decisions that can affect their lives. It is critical for the health of our democracy that the lack of diversity in political institutions of all kinds – from parliament to local government to neighbourhood forums – is addressed. Democratising citizen engagement is about recognising this glaring absence, naming it as a failure of our democracy – and doing something about it. Engaging with the already organised citizens' groups and experienced community, tenants or interest group representatives is key. But efforts to engage participation should not stop with already-existing groups or already-active individuals. Much more effort is needed to stimulate and support the representation of those who lack opportunities to be represented or to represent themselves. This can be a vital, and revitalising, *complement* to the existing system of representative democracy.

For all these efforts to generate greater democracy to succeed, the state needs to be willing to share or cede control. It needs to actively support capillary processes of democratisation that open up decision making at all levels to public engagement and scrutiny and that offer citizens a genuine chance to become part of the solution – rather than part of the problem.

## Much has changed... but much needs to change

While much has changed in the UK, there is still much that needs to change. Today we hear growing talk in policy circles of 'empowerment'. And we know that engaging those with least voice and power in our society needs to begin by providing the enabling conditions and support for them to empower themselves. But this is far more than an individual process of building the capacity to exercise choice, to which the term 'empowerment' has been reduced in international development.[94] The more radical origins of this word must not be forgotten as it becomes mainstreamed into government policy.

Empowerment is fundamentally about power. It is about transforming society through collective as well as more individual processes. It is about gaining greater control over our lives. Infusing the empowerment agenda with a strong emphasis on social justice focuses attention on transforming power relations for a more just society for all. This is a process in which state actors play an essential part in guaranteeing and protecting rights and promoting greater social, political and economic equality, at the same time as enabling citizens and communities to have more of a say in the decisions that affect their lives.

Promoting 'active citizenship' and 'empowering communities' would seem at first glance to be about the state stepping back and letting individuals and communities take more charge of their own affairs. This may call not for *less* engagement by the state but for a *shift* in the ways in which the public sector and public authorities engage with citizens. International experience suggests that short-cut approaches to empowerment rarely bring about the kind of deep-rooted changes that really make a difference to the prospects of the poorest and most marginalised people.

'Empowerment lite' may be attractive to government as it appears to promise extensive gains for minimal investment – whether in terms of small loans for micro-entrepreneurs or 'community kitties'. But thinking of empowerment within a framework of social justice and equality goes much deeper. It focuses attention on the changes that need to take place at every level in our society if poverty, social exclusion and other social ills are to be addressed. If government is genuinely committed to the longer, slower, deeper process of genuinely transformative empowerment, this may require *more* rather than less input from the state. This may come to depend as much on working *on*, *with* and *from within* the state as on efforts to engage civil society and citizens in arms' length 'community empowerment' initiatives. The enabling state still has an enormously important role to play.

## Making it real

*Can we convert optimistic rhetoric into a meaningful 'right to participate' for every citizen? And can we find a vehicle to ensure the promotion, implementation, support and scrutiny that the participation agenda deserves? Together, we believe, we can.*
Ed Cox[95]

Around the world, in the most unlikely places, pockets of innovation in governance are starting to expand. New ideas are catching on. Governments are learning that there is actually something very valuable to be gained from investing in creating the conditions for and fostering citizen engagement in governance. Exciting changes are afoot in local governments all over the UK. The political commitment seems to be there. But to make the most of this policy moment and turn the rhetoric about citizen engagement into practice, much more needs to change.

Making real the democratic promise of citizen engagement is about more than getting institutions right and inviting people to participate in them. Lessons from international experience suggest that genuine, inclusive citizen engagement requires investment in creating an enabling environment, and in supporting society's least vocal and powerful people to gain the means to use their voice. Engaging citizens can make a huge difference in designing policies that really fit with what people need and want, making the most of the knowledge and experience that citizens have of what works, and what does not. But phoney consultation does little to foster this kind of engagement, or build a sense of citizenship, ownership or empowerment. It can do precisely the opposite: put people off participating, and make them feel even more disaffected and disenfranchised.

Getting it right is critical if we are to experience the kind of democratic renewal that Britain so badly needs. In the past, there has been too much packaging pre-designed decisions and presenting them for rubber stamping and too little willingness to allow citizens and their representatives to play a more direct role in shaping and monitoring public policy. This may be the way modern democracies handle demands for public involvement, but it is not a solution to the democratic deficit. By focusing on 'ordinary' spaces for citizen engagement rather than success stories, the case studies presented here help us to get a sharper sense of what needs to be done if citizen engagement is to contribute to democracy, social inclusion and community empowerment, as well as to making governments more efficient and accountable. The difficulties and shortcomings that they illustrate provide rich material for thinking through the measures that might be needed to address these dilemmas.

What, then, might be done to democratize citizen engagement and realise its democratising promise?

### Make more of what's known about facilitating participation

A vast array of techniques and technologies exist for facilitating participation. These constitute a veritable smorgasbord of possibilities for public engagement. Whether they consist of the use of imaginative visualisation methods or simply inventive ways of running a meeting, these techniques and technologies can make a huge difference to who gets to speak and to listen. There are ways of setting up and running the kind of institutions that this pamphlet has largely focused on that make them more or less democratic and more or less effective. There are ways of doing consultations that are more or less inclusive and informative to decision makers and citizens. *It is not rocket science.* Why so much bad practice persists is not because not enough is known about how to do things better.

### Improve representation, especially of those who are least well represented in existing institutions

Democratising citizen engagement calls for bringing a greater diversity of perspectives to the table. More explicit attention needs to be paid to the selection and recruitment mechanisms that enable both state and society to be represented in all their diversity. Descriptive representation remains important for marginalised groups. But it shouldn't replace efforts to build constituencies. Nor should efforts to involve particular interest groups preclude active attempts to create the possibilities for alliances that are based less on identities than on identifying with a common agenda for social justice and equality *for all*. It is also about recognising that new democratic spaces are producing an array of new forms of representation, and being open to working with these to strengthen their democratic legitimacy and accountability.

### Bring social justice into the heart of governance

Deliberate efforts need to be made to make sure that the forms of exclusion that exist in society and in formal political institutions are not just reproduced in participatory institutions. This requires action on several fronts. It calls for support – financial, logistical as well as moral and political – so that marginalised groups can begin to organise, explore common experiences and begin to develop an agenda of their own. Community organising, consciousness-raising and popular education methods, tried and tested over decades, are powerful tools for change. They can be used to build people's sense of their own agency, and enable them to use it to exercise voice. Such tools need to be complemented by institutional designs that actively promote zero tolerance of sexism, racism, homophobia and other forms of discrimination, and permit space for different cultural forms of expression alongside those patterned by cultures of officialdom.

### Foster deliberation – not just consultation

Democratising public involvement is not only about the people, but also about the *process*. Deliberation – the exchange of reasons, views, information, evidence, through which people listen, contribute, shift their views, return to their own positions, and, together, get a broader sense of what is at stake – is a way to get fresh thinking on an issue, rather than people repeating what they have heard or been led to believe. Participatory institutions foster better deliberation if participants are provided with information and access to expertise to inform their deliberations, and encouraged to form positions during the discussions rather than to bring pre-prepared positions and agendas with them. It is where there is animated disagreement that public officials can learn the most about what matters to people. Where that disagreement can be transformed into a working consensus, it can provide the basis for legitimacy – something that is critical for the democratic exercise of authority. For this to happen, the kinds of decisions citizens are invited to participate in shaping need to be decisions that *matter* and in which they have a stake.

### Invest in building the capacity to participate – for all involved

Many participatory institutions experience a constant turnover of people, either by design or through attrition. Regular renovation of membership brings in new faces, and potentially expands democracy by releasing those with knowledge and skills acquired in these spaces to engage in others. But skills, experience and institutional memory disappear each time. To function effectively, participatory sphere institutions need infrastructure that guarantees that institutional memory is preserved, to organise and document meetings, to keep and make available documents relating to the institution's core business and to carry out other vital coordinating functions. They require that each member have a clear understanding of their role, and the role of the institution. And they require a commitment to training representatives, from the state as well as society, to equip them with the skills and knowledge to participate. This applies as much to state officials as to citizens.

### Enable public servants to serve the public better

Democratising public involvement is not only about making sure more diverse, more informed and more organised citizens are able to make their voices heard. It is also about transforming attitudes and behaviour at all levels within the public sector. This is a huge task. Part of the process of facilitating inclusive participation is to enable managers and other public officials to leave old ways behind. Public sector officials may assume that their training as professionals gives them greater understanding of the issues. They can pick up an epidemiological report or environmental assessment and skim it to pick out relevant information. But what they may be less aware of is how ordinary people see the issues. Much more effort needs to be put into working with bureaucrats and service providers at all levels to help them to generate better information about what people actually need and want.

**Strengthen the legal framework**

Lastly, while the 2007 Local Government and Public Involvement in Health Act marks an important step forward, there is a need to continue to strengthen both the legal framework and related administrative provisions. There is much that can be learnt from the legislation that has been passed in other countries, including that which contributes towards creating an enabling environment for citizen engagement, such as a right to information. This needs to be backed with the financial and administrative resources needed to make citizen engagement viable. Guidance might be sought in developing the UK's legal framework from countries that have gone significantly further in putting comprehensive enabling legislation in place, such as Brazil and India.

As the Power Inquiry put it, 'when participation meets the expectations of today's citizen, those citizens will get involved'.[96] The challenge for the UK is to meet those expectations, and to create a culture of participation that will genuinely engage its citizens. The UK could gain a lot from looking more closely at what other countries are doing and bringing some of these lessons home.

# Notes

1   Power Inquiry, *Power to the People*.

2   Skidmore and Bound, *The Everyday Democracy Index*.

3   See, for example, Mansbridge, 'On the idea that participation makes better citizens'; and www.ratifiersfordemocracy.org/HappinessandDemocracy.html (accessed 11 Apr 2008).

4   McGee with Bazaara et al, *Legal Frameworks for Citizen Participation*.

5   Power Inquiry, *Power to the People*.

6   Hansard Society, *Audit of Political Participation 5*.

7   Bentley, *Everyday Democracy*; Skidmore and Bound, *The Everyday Democracy Index*.

8   Dryzek, *Deliberative Democracy and Beyond*.

9   Gaventa, *Representation, Community Leadership and Participation*.

10   Chambers, *Whose Reality Counts?*

11   Flower et al (eds), *PLA Notes 38: Participatory Processes in the North*.

12   See for example special issues in the *PLA Notes* series: Goldman and Abbott (eds), *PLA Notes 49: Decentralisation and Community-Based Planning*; Inglis and Hesse (eds), *PLA Notes 44: Local Government and Participation*; Clark et al (eds), *PLA Notes 43: Advocacy and Citizen Participation*; and Pimbert and Wakeford (eds), *PLA Notes 40: Deliberative Democracy and Citizen Empowerment*.

13   See Dunn et al, *Champions of Participation* and supporting resources; Zipfel and Gaventa, *Citizen Participation in Local Governance*.

14  Skidmore and Bound, *The Everyday Democracy Index*.

15  Bentley, *Everyday Democracy*.

16  Case studies from this project can be found in Cornwall and Schattan Coelho (eds), 'New democratic spaces?'; and Cornwall and Schattan Coelho (eds), *Spaces for Change?*

17  See Cornwall and Schattan Coelho (eds), 'New democratic spaces?'; Gaventa, *Representation, Community Leadership and Participation*; and Cornwall and Schattan Coelho (eds), *Spaces for Change?*

18  See, for example, Goetz and Gaventa, *Bringing Citizen Voice and Client Focus into Service Delivery*; Fung and Wright, *Deepening Democracy*; Hickey and Mohan (eds), *Participation*; see also resources at www.ids.ac.uk/logolink, www.drc-citizenship.org and www.toolkitparticipation.nl (all accessed 11 Apr 2008).

19  Ribot, 'Participation without representation'; Cornwall, 'Historical perspectives on participation in development'.

20  This is precisely what Demos' everyday democracy index seeks to do. See Skidmore and Bound, *The Everyday Democracy Index*.

21  Benn, Preface to *Making Governance Work for Poor People*.

22  Fox, 'The uncertain relationship between transparency and accountability'.

23  Cohen and Sabel, 'Directly-deliberative polyarchy'.

24  Bentley, *Everyday Democracy*.

25  Arnstein, 'A ladder of citizen participation'.

26  Skidmore et al, *Community Participation*.

27  Farrington et al, *Reluctant Partners*.

28  There is a wealth of resources on participatory methodologies and
    techniques for participatory governance. See, for example,
    www.pnet.ids.ac.uk/prc/index.htm,
    www.peopleandparticipation.net/display/methods and
    www.toolkitparticipation.nl (all accessed 13 Apr 2008);
    Smith, *Beyond the Ballot*; New Economics Foundation and
    UK Participation Network, *Participation Works!* There are
    also dedicated websites for some of the methodologies
    mentioned here, including www.photovoice.com,
    www.nif.co.uk/planningforreal/,
    www.participatorybudgeting.org.uk (for UK applications),
    www.futuresearch.net, www.citizenreportcard.com,
    www.cardboardcitizens.org.uk/theatre_of_the_oppressed.php
    and http://cdd.stanford.edu/polls/docs/summary/ (all accessed
    13 Apr 2008). See also Dungey, *Citizens' Panels*; Davies et al,
    *Ordinary Wisdom*.

29  White, 'Depoliticising development'.

30  Gaventa, 'Triumph, deficit or contestation?'; Fung and Wright,
    *Deepening Democracy*.

31  Dagnino, 'Citizenship'.

32  Batliwala and Dhanraj, 'Gender myths that instrumentalise
    women'.

33  See, for example, the recent consultation paper produced by the
    Department of Communities and Local Government, 'Unlocking
    the talent of our communities'.

34  Brown, speech, 3 Jul 2007.

35  Ibid.

36  The exact language is as follows: '3A Involvement of Local
    Representatives: (1) Where a best value authority considers it
    appropriate for representatives of local persons (or of local persons
    of a particular description) to be involved in the exercise of any of
    its functions by being – (a) provided with information about the

exercise of the function; (b) consulted about the exercise of the
function, or (c) involved in another way, it must take such steps as
it considers appropriate to secure that such representatives are
involved in the exercise of the function in that way.' Much clearly
depends on what is judged appropriate by the local authority.

37  See www.communities.gov.uk/documents/communities/
    pdf/actionplan (accessed 13 Apr 2008).

38  Public perceptions of empowerment survey data, see
    www.communities.gov.uk/communities/communityempowerment/
    unlockingthetalent/ (accessed 31 Mar 2008).

39  Local and Regional Government Research Unit, *Public Participation
    in Local Government*.

40  Local and Regional Government Research Unit, *New Localism –
    Citizen Engagement, Neighbourhoods and Public Services*.

41  See Goodin and Dryzek, 'Deliberative impacts'.

42  Cornwall, *Beneficiary, Consumer, Citizen*; Brock et al, *Power, Knowledge
    and Political Spaces in the Framing of Poverty Policy*; Gaventa, 'Towards
    participatory local governance'.

43  Goetz and Gaventa, *Bringing Citizen Voice and Client Focus into Service
    Delivery*.

44  See Fung, 'Survey article: Recipes for public spheres'.

45  Ibid.

46  Goodin and Dryzek, 'Deliberative impacts'.

47  Fung, 'Survey article: Recipes for public spheres'.

48  Avritzer, *Democracy and Public Space in Latin America*.

49  Cornwall and Shankland, 'Engaging citizens'.

50 Schattan Coelho, 'Brazilian health councils'; Cornwall, 'Democratizing the governance of health services'.

51 McGee et al, *Legal Frameworks for Citizen Participation*.

52 Gaventa, *Representation, Community Leadership and Participation*.

53 Cornwall and Gaventa, *From Users and Choosers to Makers and Shapers*.

54 Chandhoke, *The Conceits of Civil Society*.

55 Williams, *Keywords*.

56 Taylor et al, 'A sea-change or a swamp?'; Gaventa, *Representation, Community Leadership and Participation*; Morris, *Removing the Barriers to Community Participation*.

57 Mahmud, 'Spaces for participation in health systems in rural Bangladesh'.

58 Jenkins and Goetz, 'Accounts and accountability'; Bose et al, 'Information as power'.

59 Gaventa, 'Towards participatory local governance'.

60 Mahmud, 'Spaces for participation in health systems in rural Bangladesh'.

61 There is a growing literature on participatory budgeting in Brazil, including studies that explore some of its political and contextual complexities. For an excellent example of this kind of work, see Baierle, 'The Porto Alegre thermidor?'.

62 Wampler, 'Does participatory democracy actually deepen democracy?'; see also Wampler, *Participatory Budgeting in Brazil*.

63 Cornwall, 'Making spaces, changing places'.

64 Houtzager et al, 'Who participates?'.

65  Norris, *Democratic Phoenix*.

66  Power, *Personal Politics*; Hansard Society, *Audit of Political Participation 5*.

67  Houtzager et al, 'Who participates?'; Castello et al, 'Civil organizations and political representation in Brazil's participatory institutions'.

68  Williams, 'Social change and community participation'.

69  Mohanty, 'Gendered subjects, the state and participatory spaces'.

70  Chaudhuri and Heller, *Plasticity of Participation*.

71  Ibid.

72  See, for example, Fishkin and Luskin, 'The quest for deliberative democracy'.

73  See, for example, Fung, 'Survey article: Recipes for public spheres'.

74  Mansbridge, 'What does a representative do?'.

75  Phillips, *Politics of Presence*.

76  Kahane and von Lieres, 'Inclusion and representation in democratic deliberations'.

77  Kohn, 'Language, power and persuasion'; Fraser, 'Rethinking the public sphere'.

78  Mansbridge, 'What does a representative do?'.

79  Interview, 9 Mar 2007.

80  Mansbridge and Morris, *Oppositional Consciousness*.

81  Mouffe, *Politics and Passions*.

82 Dryzek, 'Political inclusion and the dynamics of democratisation'.

83 Taylor et al, 'A sea-change or a swamp?'.

84 Lorde, *Sister Outsider*.

85 Batliwala and Dhanraj, 'Gender myths that instrumentalise women'.

86 Barnes, 'Whose space?'.

87 See Arnstein's ladder, referred to in chapter 2 of this pamphlet.

88 Nyamu-Musembi, 'Towards an actor-orientated perspective on human rights'.

89 Personal communication, May 2005.

90 Fraser, 'Mapping the feminist imagination'.

91 This point is also strongly made in Demos' work on everyday democracy, and is one of the conclusions from the Power Inquiry.

92 Dewey, cited in Power Inquiry, *Power to the People*.

93 Many of these factors resonate with those identified in various publications associated with the LogoLink programme, especially the work by Rosie McGee, John Gaventa, Rose Marie Nierras and their colleagues; see www.ids.ac.uk/logolink (accessed 11 Apr 2008). Similar points are made by the panel of experts consulted by the National Community Forum, in Morris, *Removing the Barriers to Community Participation*.

94 Batliwala, 'Putting power back into empowerment'.

95 Preface to Morris, *Removing the Barriers to Community Participation*.

96 Power Inquiry, *Power to the People*.

# References

Arnstein, SR, 'A ladder of citizen participation', *Journal of the American Institute of Planners* 35, no 4 (1969).

Avritzer, L, *Democracy and Public Space in Latin America* (Princeton: Princeton University Press, 2002).

Baierle, S, 'The Porto Alegre thermidor? Brazil's "participatory budget" at the crossroads', *Socialist Register* (2003).

Barnes, M, 'Whose space? Contestations and negotiations in health and community regeneration fora in the UK' in Cornwall and Schattan Coelho (eds), *Spaces for Change?*.

Batliwala, S, 'Putting power back into empowerment', *Open Democracy*, 2007, available at www.opendemocracy.net/article/putting_power_back_into_empowerment_0 (accessed 11 Apr 2008).

Batliwala, S and Dhanraj, D, 'Gender myths that instrumentalise women: a view from the Indian frontline', *IDS Bulletin* 35, no 4 (2004).

Benn, H, Preface to *Making Governance Work for Poor People* (London: Department for International Development, 2006).

Bentley, T, *Everyday Democracy: Why we get the politicians we deserve* (London: Demos, 2005).

Bose, S, Lal, P and Saigal, S, 'Information as power: making best use of India's Right to Information law' in Vermeulen (ed), *PLA Notes 53: Tools for Influencing Power and Policy*.

Brock, K, Cornwall, A and Gaventa, J, *Power, Knowledge and Political Spaces in the Framing of Poverty Policy* (Brighton: Institute of Development Studies, 2001).

Brown, G, speech, 3 Jul 2007, see 'Brown on constitution', available at http://news.bbc.co.uk/1/hi/uk_politics/6266526.stm (accessed 31 Mar 2008).

Calhoun, C (ed), *Habermas and the Public Sphere* (Cambridge, MA: MIT Press, 1992).

Castello, G, Lavalle, A and Houtzager, P, 'Civil organizations and political representation in Brazil's participatory institutions' in Cornwall and Schattan Coelho (eds), *Spaces for Change?*.

Chambers, R, *Whose Reality Counts? Putting the first last* (London: Intermediate Technology Publications, 1997).

Chandhoke, N, *The Conceits of Civil Society* (New Delhi: Oxford University Press, 2003).

Chaudhuri, S and Heller, P, *The Plasticity of Participation: Evidence from a participatory governance experiment* (New York: Columbia University, 2002).

Clark, C et al (eds), *PLA Notes 43: Advocacy and Citizen Participation* (London: International Institute for Environment and Development, 2002).

Cohen, J and Sabel, C, 'Directly-deliberative polyarchy', *European Law Journal* 3, no 4 (1997).

Cornwall, A, *Beneficiary, Consumer, Citizen: Perspectives on participation for poverty reduction* (Stockholm: Sida Studies, 2000).

Cornwall, A, 'Democratizing the governance of health services: the case of Cabo de Santo Agostinho, Brazil' in Cornwall and Schattan Coelho (eds), *Spaces for Change?*.

Cornwall, A, 'Historical perspectives on participation in development', *Journal of Comparative and Commonwealth Politics* 44, no 1 (2006).

Cornwall, A, 'Making spaces, changing places: situating participation in development', IDS Working Paper 170 (Brighton: Institute of Development Studies, 2002).

Cornwall, A, 'Spaces for transformation? Reflections on issues of power and difference in participation in development' in Hickey and Mohan (eds), *Participation*.

Cornwall, A and Gaventa, J, *From Users and Choosers to Makers and Shapers: Repositioning participation in social policy* (Brighton: Institute of Development Studies, 2001).

Cornwall, A and Schattan Coelho, V (eds), 'New democratic spaces? The politics of institutionalized participation', *IDS Bulletin* 35, no 2 (2004).

Cornwall, A and Schattan Coelho, V (eds), *Spaces for Change? The politics of citizen participation in new democratic arenas* (London: Zed Books, 2007).

Cornwall, A and Shankland, A, 'Engaging citizens: lessons from building Brazil's national health system', *Social Science and Medicine* (10 Mar 2008, e-publication ahead of print).

Dagnino, E, 'Citizenship: a perverse confluence', *Development in Practice* 17, no 4&5 (2007).

Davies, S et al, *Ordinary Wisdom: Reflections on an experiment in citizenship and health* (London: King's Fund, 1998).

Department of Communities and Local Government, 'Unlocking the talent of our communities', Mar 2008, available at www.communities.gov.uk/communities/communityempowerment/ unlockingthetalent/ (accessed 13 April 2008).

Dryzek, JS, *Deliberative Democracy and Beyond: Liberals, critics, contestations* (Oxford: Oxford University Press, 2000).

Dryzek, JS, 'Political inclusion and the dynamics of democratisation', *American Political Science Review* 90, no 3 (1996).

Dungey, J, *Citizens' Panels* (London: Local Government Information Unit, 1997).

Dunn, A et al, *Champions of Participation: Engaging citizens in local governance* (2007), available at www.ids.ac.uk/logolink (accessed 12 Apr 2008).

Elkin, S and Soltan, KE (eds), *Citizen Competence and Democratic Institutions* (University Park, PA: Penn State University Press, 1999).

Farrington, J and Bebbington, AJ with Wellard, K and Lewis, DI, *Reluctant Partners: Non-governmental organisations, the state and sustainable agricultural development in Latin America* (London: Routledge, 1993).

Fishkin, J and Luskin, R, 'The quest for deliberative democracy', *The Good Society* 9, no 1 (1999).

Flower, C, Mincher, P and Rimkus, S (eds), *PLA Notes 38: Participatory Processes in the North* (London: International Institute for Environment and Development, 2000).

Fox, J, 'The uncertain relationship between transparency and accountability', *Development in Practice* 17, no 4&5 (2007).

Fraser, N, 'Mapping the feminist imagination: from redistribution to recognition to representation', *Constellations* 12, no 3 (2005).

Fraser, N, 'Rethinking the public sphere: a contribution to the critique of actually existing democracy' in Calhoun (ed), *Habermas and the Public Sphere*.

Fung, A, 'Survey article: Recipes for public spheres: eight institutional design choices and their consequences', *Journal of Political Philosophy* 11, no 3 (2003).

Fung, A and Wright, EO, *Deepening Democracy: Institutional innovations in empowered participatory governance* (London: Verso, 2003).

Gaventa, J, *Representation, Community Leadership and Participation: Citizen involvement in neighbourhood renewal and local governance* (Brighton: Institute of Development Studies and Logolink, 2004).

Gaventa, J, 'Towards participatory local governance: assessing the transformative possibilities' in Hickey and Mohan (eds), *Participation*.

Gaventa, J, 'Triumph, deficit or contestation? Deepening the "deepening democracy" debate', IDS Working Paper 264 (Brighton: Institute of Development Studies, 2006).

Goetz, AM and Gaventa, J, *Bringing Citizen Voice and Client Focus into Service Delivery* (Brighton: Institute of Development Studies, 2001).

Goldman, I and Abbott, J (eds), *PLA Notes 49: Decentralisation and Community-Based Planning* (London: International Institute for Environment and Development, 2004).

Goodin, RE and Dryzek, JS, 'Deliberative impacts: the macro-political uptake of mini-publics', *Politics & Society* 34 (2006).

Hansard Society, *Audit of Political Participation 5* (London: Hansard Society and Electoral Commission, March 2008).

Hickey, S and Mohan, G (eds), *Participation: From tyranny to transformation?* (London: Zed Books, 2004).

Houtzager, P, Lavalle, AG and Acharya, A, 'Who participates? Civil society and the new democratic politics in São Paulo, Brazil', IDS Working Paper 210 (Brighton: Institute of Development Studies, 2003).

Inglis, A and Hesse, C (eds), *PLA Notes 44: Local Government and Participation* (London: International Institute for Environment and Development, 2002).

Jenkins, R and Goetz, AM, 'Accounts and accountability: theoretical implications for the right-to-information movement in India', *Third World Quarterly* 20, no 3 (1999).

Kabeer, N (ed), *Inclusive Citizenship: Meanings and expressions* (London: Zed Books, 2005).

Kahane, D and von Lieres, B, 'Inclusion and representation in democratic deliberations: lessons from Canada's Romanow Commission' in Cornwall and Schattan Coelho (eds), *Spaces for Change?*.

Kohn, M, 'Language, power and persuasion: toward a critique of deliberative democracy', *Constellations* 7, no 3 (2000).

Kymlicka, W and Norman, W (eds), *Citizenship in Diverse Societies* (Oxford: Oxford University Press, 2000).

Local and Regional Government Research Unit, *New Localism – Citizen Engagement, Neighbourhoods and Public Services: Evidence from local government* (London: Office of the Deputy Prime Minister, 2005).

Local and Regional Government Research Unit, *Public Participation in Local Government: A survey of local authorities* (London: Office of the Deputy Prime Minister, 2002).

Lorde, A, *Sister Outsider* (Trumansburg, NY: The Crossing Press, 1984).

Mahmud, S, 'Spaces for participation in health systems in rural Bangladesh: the experience of stakeholder community groups' in Cornwall and Schattan Coelho (eds), *Spaces for Change?*.

Mansbridge, J, 'On the idea that participation makes better citizens' in Elkin and Soltan (eds), *Citizen Competence and Democratic Institutions*.

Mansbridge, J, 'What does a representative do? Descriptive representation in communicative settings of distrust, uncrystallized interests, and historically denigrated status' in Kymlicka and Norman (eds), *Citizenship in Diverse Societies*.

Mansbridge, J and Morris, A, *Oppositional Consciousness: The subjective roots of social protest* (Chicago: University of Chicago Press, 2001).

McGee, R with Bazaara, N et al, *Legal Frameworks for Citizen Participation: Synthesis report* (Brighton: Logolink and Institute of Development Studies, 2003).

Mohanty, R, 'Gendered subjects, the state and participatory spaces: the politics of domesticating participation in rural India' in Cornwall and Schattan Coelho (eds), *Spaces for Change?*.

Morris, J, *Removing the Barriers to Community Participation* (London: National Community Forum, 2006), available at www.communities.gov.uk/documents/communities/pdf/621189 (accessed 11 Apr 2008).

Mouffe, C, *Politics and Passions: The states of democracy* (London: Centre for the Study of Democracy, 2002).

New Economics Foundation and UK Participation Network, *Participation Works! 21 techniques of community participation for the 21st century* (London: New Economics Foundation, 1998).

Norris, P, *Democratic Phoenix* (Cambridge: Cambridge University Press, 2002).

Nyamu-Musembi, C, 'Towards an actor-orientated perspective on human rights' in Kabeer (ed), *Inclusive Citizenship*.

Phillips, A, *The Politics of Presence* (Oxford: Oxford University Press, 1995).

Pimbert, M and Wakeford, T (eds), *PLA Notes 40: Deliberative Democracy and Citizen Empowerment* (London: International Institute for Environment and Development, 2001).

Power, G, *Personal Politics: Democracy, participation and collective action* (London: Carnegie Trust, 2006).

Power Inquiry, *Power to the People: The report of Power: an independent inquiry into Britain's democracy* (London: Power Inquiry, 2006), available at www.makeitanissue.org.uk/ Power%20to%20the%20People.pdf (accessed 11 Apr 2008).

Ribot, J, 'Participation without representation: chiefs, councils and forestry law in the West African Sahel', *Cultural Survival Quarterly* (Fall 1996).

Schattan Coelho, V, 'Brazilian health councils: including the excluded?' in Cornwall and Schattan Coelho (eds), *Spaces for Change?*.

Skidmore, P and Bound, K, *The Everyday Democracy Index* (London: Demos, 2008).

Skidmore, P, Bound, K and Lownsbrough, H, *Community Participation: Who benefits?* (York: Joseph Rowntree Foundation, 2006).

Smith, G, *Beyond the Ballot: 57 Democratic innovations from around the world* (London: Power Inquiry, 2005), available at www.makeitanissue.org.uk/Beyond%20the%20Ballot.pdf (accessed 11 Apr 2008).

Taylor, M with Craig, G et al, 'A sea-change or a swamp? New spaces for voluntary sector engagement in governance in the UK', *IDS Bulletin* 35, no 2 (2004).

Vermeulen, S (ed), *PLA Notes 53: Tools for Influencing Power and Policy* (London: International Institute for Environment and Development, 2005).

Wampler, B, 'Does participatory democracy actually deepen democracy? Lessons from Brazil', 2008, available at www.internationalbudget.org/themes/PB/ParticipatoryInstitutions. pdf (accessed 14 Apr 2008).

Wampler, B, *Participatory Budgeting in Brazil: Contestation, cooperation, and accountability* (University Park, PA: Penn State University Press, 2007), available at www.psupress.org/books/titles/978-0-271-03252-8.html (accessed 15 Apr 2008).

White, S, 'Depoliticising development: the uses and abuses of participation', *Development in Practice* 6, no 1 (1996).

Williams, J, 'Social change and community participation: the case of health facilities boards in the Western Cape of South Africa' in Cornwall and Schattan Coelho (eds), *Spaces for Change?*.

Williams, R, *Keywords* (London: Picador, 1976).

Zipfel, T and Gaventa, J, *Citizen Participation in Local Governance*, policy brief (Brighton: Institute of Development Studies, 2008).

# Demos – Licence to Publish

The work (as defined below) is provided under the terms of this licence ('licence'). The work is protected by copyright and/or other applicable law. Any use of the work other than as authorized under this licence is prohibited. By exercising any rights to the work provided here, you accept and agree to be bound by the terms of this licence. Demos grants you the rights contained here in consideration of your acceptance of such terms and conditions.

## 1 Definitions

A  **'Collective Work'** means a work, such as a periodical issue, anthology or encyclopedia, in which the Work in its entirety in unmodified form, along with a number of other contributions, constituting separate and independent works in themselves, are assembled into a collective whole. A work that constitutes a Collective Work will not be considered a Derivative Work (as defined below) for the purposes of this Licence.

B  **'Derivative Work'** means a work based upon the Work or upon the Work and other pre-existing works, such as a musical arrangement, dramatization, fictionalization, motion picture version, sound recording, art reproduction, abridgment, condensation, or any other form in which the Work may be recast, transformed, or adapted, except that a work that constitutes a Collective Work or a translation from English into another language will not be considered a Derivative Work for the purpose of this Licence.

C  **'Licensor'** means the individual or entity that offers the Work under the terms of this Licence.

D  **'Original Author'** means the individual or entity who created the Work.

E  **'Work'** means the copyrightable work of authorship offered under the terms of this Licence.

F  **'You'** means an individual or entity exercising rights under this Licence who has not previously violated the terms of this Licence with respect to the Work,or who has received express permission from Demos to exercise rights under this Licence despite a previous violation.

## 2 Fair Use Rights

Nothing in this licence is intended to reduce, limit, or restrict any rights arising from fair use, first sale or other limitations on the exclusive rights of the copyright owner under copyright law or other applicable laws.

## 3 Licence Grant

Subject to the terms and conditions of this Licence, Licensor hereby grants You a worldwide, royalty-free, non-exclusive,perpetual (for the duration of the applicable copyright) licence to exercise the rights in the Work as stated below:

A  to reproduce the Work, to incorporate the Work into one or more Collective Works, and to reproduce the Work as incorporated in the Collective Works;

B  to distribute copies or phonorecords of, display publicly,perform publicly, and perform publicly by means of a digital audio transmission the Work including as incorporated in Collective Works; The above rights may be exercised in all media and formats whether now known or hereafter devised.The above rights include the right to make such modifications as are technically necessary to exercise the rights in other media and formats. All rights not expressly granted by Licensor are hereby reserved.

## 4 Restrictions

The licence granted in Section 3 above is expressly made subject to and limited by the following restrictions:

A  You may distribute,publicly display, publicly perform, or publicly digitally perform the Work only under the terms of this Licence, and You must include a copy of, or the Uniform Resource Identifier for, this Licence with every copy or phonorecord of the Work You distribute, publicly display,publicly perform, or publicly digitally perform.You may not offer or impose any terms on the Work that alter or restrict the terms of this Licence or the recipients' exercise of the rights granted hereunder.You may not sublicence the Work.You must keep intact all notices that refer to this Licence and to the disclaimer of warranties.You may not distribute, publicly display, publicly perform, or publicly digitally perform the Work with any technological measures that control access or use of the Work in a manner inconsistent with the terms of this Licence Agreement.The above applies to the Work as incorporated in a Collective Work, but this does not require the Collective Work apart from the Work itself to be made subject to the terms of this Licence. If You create a Collective Work, upon notice from any Licencor You must, to the extent practicable, remove from the Collective Work any reference to such Licensor or the Original Author, as requested.

B  You may not exercise any of the rights granted to You in Section 3 above in any manner that is primarily intended for or directed toward commercial advantage or private monetary compensation.The exchange of the Work for other copyrighted works by means of digital filesharing or otherwise shall not be considered to be intended for or directed toward commercial advantage or private monetary compensation, provided there is no payment of any monetary compensation in connection with the exchange of copyrighted works.

c   If you distribute, publicly display, publicly perform, or publicly digitally perform the Work or any Collective Works,You must keep intact all copyright notices for the Work and give the Original Author credit reasonable to the medium or means You are utilizing by conveying the name (or pseudonym if applicable) of the Original Author if supplied; the title of the Work if supplied. Such credit may be implemented in any reasonable manner; provided, however, that in the case of a Collective Work, at a minimum such credit will appear where any other comparable authorship credit appears and in a manner at least as prominent as such other comparable authorship credit.

## 5   Representations, Warranties and Disclaimer

A   By offering the Work for public release under this Licence, Licensor represents and warrants that, to the best of Licensor's knowledge after reasonable inquiry:

i   Licensor has secured all rights in the Work necessary to grant the licence rights hereunder and to permit the lawful exercise of the rights granted hereunder without You having any obligation to pay any royalties, compulsory licence fees, residuals or any other payments;

ii  The Work does not infringe the copyright, trademark, publicity rights, common law rights or any other right of any third party or constitute defamation, invasion of privacy or other tortious injury to any third party.

B   except as expressly stated in this licence or otherwise agreed in writing or required by applicable law,the work is licenced on an 'as is'basis,without warranties of any kind, either express or implied including,without limitation,any warranties regarding the contents or accuracy of the work.

## 6   Limitation on Liability

Except to the extent required by applicable law, and except for damages arising from liability to a third party resulting from breach of the warranties in section 5, in no event will licensor be liable to you on any legal theory for any special, incidental,consequential, punitive or exemplary damages arising out of this licence or the use of the work, even if licensor has been advised of the possibility of such damages.

## 7   Termination

A   This Licence and the rights granted hereunder will terminate automatically upon any breach by You of the terms of this Licence. Individuals or entities who have received Collective Works from You under this Licence,however, will not have their licences terminated provided such individuals or entities remain in full compliance with those licences. Sections 1, 2, 5, 6, 7, and 8 will survive any termination of this Licence.

B   Subject to the above terms and conditions, the licence granted here is perpetual (for the duration of the applicable copyright in the Work). Notwithstanding the above, Licensor reserves the right to release the Work under different licence terms or to stop distributing the Work at any time; provided, however that any such election will not serve to withdraw this Licence (or any other licence that has been, or is required to be, granted under the terms of this Licence), and this Licence will continue in full force and effect unless terminated as stated above.

## 8   Miscellaneous

A   Each time You distribute or publicly digitally perform the Work or a Collective Work, Demos offers to the recipient a licence to the Work on the same terms and conditions as the licence granted to You under this Licence.

B   If any provision of this Licence is invalid or unenforceable under applicable law, it shall not affect the validity or enforceability of the remainder of the terms of this Licence, and without further action by the parties to this agreement, such provision shall be reformed to the minimum extent necessary to make such provision valid and enforceable.

C   No term or provision of this Licence shall be deemed waived and no breach consented to unless such waiver or consent shall be in writing and signed by the party to be charged with such waiver or consent.

D   This Licence constitutes the entire agreement between the parties with respect to the Work licensed here.There are no understandings, agreements or representations with respect to the Work not specified here. Licensor shall not be bound by any additional provisions that may appear in any communication from You.This Licence may not be modified without the mutual written agreement of Demos and You.